You Had Me At No

How Setting Healthy Boundaries
Banishes Burnout,
Repairs Relationships, and
Saves Your Sanity

Dear Drew,
Happy Boundary
Setting !

♡

Sheryl Green

By
Sheryl Green

This book is dedicated to the people-pleasers, the codependents, and anyone who has ever said yes when they wanted to say no.

You are my people, and I've got your back.

Contents

Part 3: Boundary Reflections

Introduction

I hate Monopoly.

No offense to that little dog or the top hat. I've even got a Muppet Monopoly set and, heaven knows, I love Muppets. It's just that if you asked anyone who knows me to describe my personality, the word "capitalist" would never come up. Not even once. All the buying and selling. The shrewdness of making people give up their last dollar because they landed on your property and have to pay "rent." I don't want to put up hotels! I want to put up animal shelters and let my friends crash on my couch instead of going bankrupt. But, Milton Bradley did not have me in mind when he created this friggin' game.

So why then did I find myself surrounded by good friends and my fiance, people who love and care about my well-being, staring out a window onto the beautiful harbor of Shelter Island at 42 years of age, positioned to Pass Go and Collect $200?

No, I'm not a masochist. I'm not even a board game junkie. What I am is a recovering people-pleaser. I was playing Monopoly on that beautiful summer evening because I didn't know how to say, "Hey guys, I actually can't stand this game. Could we maybe play some cards or charades?"

Maybe you're sitting here reading this and wondering why I couldn't stand up for myself. Maybe you're reading this and wondering what I could possibly have against Monopoly (I mean, it also takes FOREVER)… but, more than likely, if you picked up this book, you've got your own "Monopoly." There are areas of your life where you've neglected to say no, to stand up for yourself, to express your needs, your likes, or your dislikes. Maybe you've even spent your entire life living up to someone else's (and probably several someones) expectations, putting yourself out to make other people happy, and afraid that if you don't make them happy, they'll leave you.

Trust me—I've been there. I've self-diagnosed with "If I don't give people what they want, they won't like me-itis," and thankfully, I'm in remission.

While you may think that being a people-pleaser is a good thing, it's not. It fosters resentment and puts a strain on everyone involved. The only way to create healthy relationships is with healthy boundaries.

If you've ever seen the movie *Jerry Maguire*, you've heard the iconic line uttered by Renee Zellweger, "You had me at hello."

Well, when you establish (and maintain) boundaries, you'll earn the respect and appreciation of others with the word "No."

Throughout this book, you're going to learn that saying no is actually a gift to yourself and to those around you. You're going to learn why you've felt compelled to "devote" your life to others and most importantly how to stop.

Before we get any further, I want to assure you that this book is not a big middle finger to the world. As you'll learn over the next two-hundred-and-something pages, I've drawn strength through helping others and I truly believe our purpose on this Earth is to serve. However, what I've also learned over the years is when it comes at the expense of our mental health, our peace, and our self-respect, we've gone too far. There's a happy medium between giving *of* yourself and giving *up* yourself, and I've been working for a long time to find it.

We teach people how to treat us. In *Once Upon a Time: Harnessing the Power of Storytelling in Sales*, I made a point regarding branding in business and in your personal life. Our brand isn't just who we tell people we are, it's who we show up as every day. In essence, we are training people to recognize us. I'm a huge animal advocate. I love dogs and while I was actively involved in rescue, my social media feeds were plastered with adoptable dogs and cats. I was constantly "telling" people how much I cared about pets. So what would've happened if I'd shown up to a party one day wearing a Cruella DeVille-esque coat made of puppy dog tails? Brand identity destroyed. (Don't worry, I would NEVER!) Remember, your actions can either bolster or undermine your words.

Swiss psychiatrist and founder of analytical psychology, Carl Jung, said, "The world will ask you who you are, and if you don't know, the world will tell you."

I say the world will ask how to treat you. If you don't know, the world will similarly decide on its own.

If you don't teach people how you want to be treated, they'll make up their own rules. If you don't reinforce it constantly, they'll slide back into whatever is most convenient for them. And, when you spend too much of your time doing for others, living for others, and focusing on others, you lose a piece of yourself. Over time, the quality of your life and your relationships deteriorate. The resentment builds inside you, and you become someone you never expected to see in the mirror.

Or… you learn to stand up for yourself.

If you hadn't guessed it yet and are currently scrunching your eyes and scratching an imaginary (or real) beard, we are talking about boundaries.

There is a place, both physical and emotional, where other people end and you begin. That place is sacred, and for many of us, it's a place we never knew existed. Cue the rainbows and the unicorns with cotton candy for manes, (don't worry, it never rains here... that would make for a very sticky unicorn). Boundaries are a magical phenomenon where your mental health improves, you gain respect from others and develop it for yourself, and you identify the relationships worth pursuing while finding the strength to release the rest.

We'll get into a more scientific definition of boundaries in a little bit. For now, I just want you to feel hope. There's a better future on the horizon and wherever you are right now is just perfect.

About the Author

At this point, you're probably wondering *who is this woman and what does she know about unicorns?*

I'm glad you asked. I'm you.

I'm not *actually* you, but I've struggled with boundaries my entire life. Hell, until a few years ago, I didn't even know what they were. I was raised to be a caretaker: to put others' needs before my own, and to put myself in other people's shoes, to constantly be concerned with their emotional state. Does this sound familiar?

As a teenage goth, I was obsessed with serial killers. When my mom told me about Profiling, my interest peaked. I was in the midst of getting an undergrad degree in Psychology and Anthropology, and while I knew I wanted to study the behavior of the individual (psychology), or the behavior of mankind (anthropology), I wasn't quite sure how. When my mom told me about Profiling, I was off to the races. So, I could study serial killers for a living… and put myself not only in their shoes but in their brains? Cue the excited squeals of a tween at her first New Kids on the Block concert.

I applied. I interviewed. And a year later, I was on my way to a Master's in Forensic Psychology. I never worked in the field. It was a huge disappointment at the time, but probably for the best in the long run. I used my degree (part of it, at least) to work in an outpatient facility for the severely mentally ill. I saw people day in and day out who had no concept of boundaries, theirs or others, who suffered greatly.

Ironically, I had no concept either.

That became really obvious (to others—I was still fricking clueless) in my next evolution. I'd been involved in animal rescue for years at that point. Truthfully, it's what pulled me from the depths of depression in my late twenties. (I told you I'm a huge advocate of serving others!) After years of volunteering and serving on a board of directors, I left my job at the mental health facility to work full-time for the animal rescue. It was a dream come true. Until it wasn't. I found the perfect environment to embrace a complete and utter lack of boundaries. After all, "it was for the animals!" I sacrificed my time, my finances, and my emotional well-being in the name of service. Stay tuned to find out how well that turned out. Spoiler alert - "dumpster fire" would be sugarcoating it.

Look, I'm not a therapist. While I have a Master's in psychology, I'm not trained, nor have I ever practiced, as a LMFT (Licensed Marriage and Family Therapist). There are a lot of books out there written by therapists (I think I've read them all at this point), and they can bring the "I've been sitting across from people with boundary issues every day for 20 years" perspective.

I bring you a different perspective. I'm trained in life. I've spent years identifying my deficiencies and working to improve them. The moment it became obvious that I sucked in the boundary department, I set my sights on a better version of myself. Yup, the kind that gets to ride around on that unicorn. I read everything I could. I consulted therapists. I interviewed the women in my life who are boundary rock stars, some of whom you will hear from later in the book. And I did A LOT of inner work. Like, A LOT.

Something cool happened. I developed boundaries. I learned to check in with myself before blurting out "Of course, I want to skip my vacation to help you finish a project you've been putting off for months," to determine whether I'm saying yes out of imagined obligation or out of a loving desire to help.

Am I perfect? Only in my dogs' eyes. Actually, I just looked over and realized I haven't fed them yet, so I'm getting the side eye from the little one. Anyhoo, I've still got a lot of work to do. But, I'm on the path to recovery. I've cleared the chasm of suckage and now it's time to hold out my hand and help you through it. Think of this as my damaged inner child talking to yours.

How To Use This Book

This book is designed to give you an overview of boundaries and how adopting healthy boundaries can improve your life. In order to do this, I've divided it into three parts.

In the first part, you will gain a strong understanding of what boundaries are and the problems you may be experiencing without them. We'll talk about where boundaries come from (or don't come from) and work through why they are more difficult to establish and uphold with some people than with others.

In part two, you'll learn how to make decisions from a place of love and strength, rather than a place of fear and weakness. We'll dive into communicating your boundaries and discuss why it's so important to surround yourself with people who respect your boundaries and have some of their own.

In part three, we'll take a look at what may happen when you set boundaries. When you are finished with this book, you will be able to identify the places (and people) in your life where you need better boundaries. You'll know how to communicate those boundaries clearly and kindly, identify where you've got more work to do, and when it's time to celebrate.

And, hopefully, you'll laugh along the way. Life is messy. Boundary work is messy. It's filled with a lot of "oopsies;" but we are going to get through this together.

It takes a village.

As I was writing this book, I reached out to some of the smartest people I know - people that are crushing boundary-setting in their personal and professional lives. I had them weigh in with their "learning to set boundaries" stories and practical tips that you can put into action today. You'll find their interviews scattered throughout the book.

A word of caution…

I know how tempting it is to read through a book and skip the exercises with an, "It's okay, I'll totally go back to them afterward." Trust me… you won't. How do I know that? Because I've been reading personal development books my entire life and I have never once "gone back afterward." Not even once. I told you—I'm you.

Do. The. Work.

When you get to the end of a chapter, you'll find a "Back to You" section. Grab a journal, read the exercise, and do the damn work. And, by the way, lest you feel the compulsion to bounce around the chapters all willy-nilly, don't. Each chapter is going to build on the last one and, if you try to skip around, you'll be unprepared, get confused, and your brain may go all kaflooey. Seriously… we don't want kaflooey brains. It's messy.

Take a moment and visit www.YouHadMeAtNo.com to download some helpful materials and worksheets that will help you along this journey.

My last piece of advice is, whatever you do, do not walk up to your loved ones and announce, "Bitches, I'm gettin' me some boundaries!"

Terri Cole advised against this in her book, *Boundary Boss,* and guess who didn't listen? Oh yeah, I'll be sharing the good, the bad, and the, "it's so ugly, you wouldn't let it out of the basement at night," of my boundary journey. I did this. I marched up to my parents, whom I love very much, and let out a Braveheart-worthy warrior cry of boundaries. Let's just say it was not received well.

Work on you. When you do this right, people will notice a (good) change in you. You won't actually have to tell them.

A few years ago, I was driving to the radio station to host my radio show, *Something to Chew On*. I was driving along a local highway minding my own business, when someone threw a rock off the overpass. I swerved to avoid the rock, but because of the amount of gravel on the road, I lost control of the car, swerving in and out of lanes until the car became airborne. My car rolled five times before coming to a stop: upright, facing the wrong direction.

It just so happens that the car closest to me was an off-duty firefighter. By the time my car uprighted itself, he had already called in the accident, and he was standing by my side window, holding my neck steady until the paramedics arrived. I was carted off to UMC Hospital, the only Level One Trauma Center in Nevada, where they ran every test imaginable.

After four hours of x-rays, MRIs, poking, prodding, stitches, and staples, I was released with aches and a concussion.

The next morning, my boyfriend at the time was heading to the junkyard to clean out what was left of my car. "I have to go with you," I said. "That car gave its life for me. The least I can do is say goodbye."

With a nod of acceptance from my parents, he loaded me into his truck, and we headed out to the junkyard. The worker was helping someone else when we walked in, so he had us take a seat in the office.

Apparently, he had passed by my car with the other customer, who promptly exclaimed, "Holy shit, that person didn't make it."

"That person is sitting in the office right now," he said.

When they came back into the office, the customer walked over to me and said, "Your car is fuuuuucked up."

Friend, your boundaries are fuuuucked up. You've been through trauma. You're bruised, battered, and likely have some scars. But, you're not broken. You can have a happy life filled with healthy boundaries and people that respect you. And, I'm going to show you how.

If you're with me, let's dive in. Let's start your journey to intentional decision-making. Right after I feed the dogs.

Part 1: Understand Boundaries

(And Why Yours are F'd Up)

Chapter 1:

Why Am I Angry, Resentful, and Exhausted?

It was late November 2021 and I'd been working, (in varying capacities), with a local animal rescue for eight-plus years. I was driving across town in the early evening to run an errand after work. Tears were streaming down my face, an occurrence I'd become very accustomed to throughout the previous months. I was driving Eastbound and despite trying to focus on the road ahead of me, I became mesmerized by the headlights of the cars driving Westbound past me.

My thoughts quickly began to drift. *It would be so easy. I could just hop this low median, and let the oncoming cars...*

I've never been so afraid of my own thoughts. And trust me, they've been dark in the past. Even in the midst of that clinical depression in my late twenties, I never had active thoughts of suicide. I wouldn't have complained if a truck or an asteroid took me out, but I certainly wasn't considering doing the deed myself.

The realization forced me to pull off the road and pull myself together. I could've hurt myself. I could've hurt someone else. What in the actual Hell was I thinking? It was an official wake-up call since, obviously, my internal alarms weren't cutting it. I needed to make some big changes in my life or I probably wasn't going to see my next birthday.

Some days my phone would ding from 6 am, while I tried to focus on my yoga practice, till 11 pm, as I attempted to decompress and sleep. Phone calls came while I was out on dates, having dinner with my parents or friends, in the shower, on the weekend, on holidays, and while I was working on the freelance projects I needed to supplement my salary so I could keep a roof over my head and kibble in my dogs' bowls. I'd start out my day with a plan and enough time to do everything. It would be quickly hijacked with "great ideas," "must do's," and last-minute emergency situations.

I'm not blaming anyone else. My phone has an off switch. It's even got a Do Not Disturb function (who knew???). Unfortunately, I, personally, did not have that same function. I was a paid employee with the right and the ability to work the hours I was paid for and then enjoy my life guilt-free. I was not an indentured servant. But... it was for the animals! I couldn't say no to them and I couldn't say no to my boss—or to any of the other demands on my time and my energy.

It reminded me of the opening scene in Arianna Huffington's *Thrive*. Sure, I wasn't running a global communications company or gracing the cover of *Time* magazine (yet!), but I had created a life I didn't want to live and I was struggling to keep my head above water. My world and my priorities were no longer my own and they were about to come crashing down.

Have you had your own "oncoming traffic" moment? Do you wake up each morning dreading the expectations and responsibilities that will be hurled at your head and will fall on your shoulders? Your boss, coworkers, kids, parents, significant others, siblings, friends, committee members, board chairs, and volunteer coordinators. The list goes on and on. It seems like everyone you know has a demand on your time. You've taken on other people's agendas, emotions, priorities, and opinions as your own. Emotional well-being and self-care are now foreign words and you feel as if the weight of the world is on you.

And hopefully, you're fed up.

Between the crying bouts… who am I kidding? I didn't stop crying for two months; go ahead, ask my friends and family. *In the midst* of crying, I realized that if I didn't start focusing on myself, I wouldn't be around to help the people and animals I cared about.

I emailed my boss and told her I had one foot on a mental breakdown and the other one on a banana peel. I gathered everything I was working on, shared all of my contacts, delegated all of my responsibilities, and apologized profusely. I told her I was taking the month of December off to protect my sanity. I didn't know how I was going to pay my bills, but I also knew it wouldn't matter if I stayed on this path.

It wasn't the first boundary I erected. It wasn't even the one that made me realize I had a lesson to learn and to share with the world. But it was probably the most important boundary I have ever, or will ever, set.

I mentioned it in the Introduction, but it bears repeating. Boundaries do not mean shutting out the world or being a selfish, self-centered, a-hole who doesn't think about anyone besides him or herself. (Okay, maybe I didn't put it *that* way in the Introduction.) Boundaries are not a tool of exclusion. They are a tool to restore (and maintain) balance in your life. They are necessary to make space for helping others, having compassion, and still taking time to care for yourself and have your own needs met.

Oh yeah, you have needs. (Don't worry, I didn't realize I did either.) You've just never given yourself permission to have them. When you are so busy focusing on meeting everyone else's needs, you get lost in the shuffle. There's only so much time in a day, and when you're too focused on other people's priorities, you don't have the resources to fulfill your own.

In *Four Thousand Weeks*, Oliver Burkeman talks about the inherent choice we make in every moment of our short time here on Earth. With only four thousand weeks on this planet, we simply won't have time to do everything. This makes choosing what we will spend our time on, even more important! With limited resources (time, money, bandwidth), whenever we choose to do something, we are also making a choice *not* to do something else.

We'll discuss resources in a later chapter. For now, I need you to answer one question: what matters most to you?

Back to You

Alright, it's time to roll up your sleeves and start digging through the recesses of your psyche. Grab a nice journal or use the back of discarded printer paper like I do, (We must protect the trees!). Find a quiet place to work or pop in some earbuds and play instrumental music. If it makes you happy, light a candle or some incense. This is your time.

Ask yourself:

1. Have I ever experienced an "oncoming traffic moment"?
2. If so, how did I feel about it?
3. Do I know what caused it or what led to it?

Sit with this for a little while and feel what you need to feel. While it's okay to feel sad or scared, if you are thinking about harming yourself or others, please contact a licensed therapist who can provide the support you need.

Chapter 2:

What Are Boundaries?

Working at the rescue, I had a number of different responsibilities across different areas. After explaining the weight of my workload, my boss encouraged me to choose someone who could help me; I knew just the person.

My friend Jamie has been a devoted animal lover and rescuer for decades. She had a wide skill set, was eager to help, and needed a part-time job after she retired from her position with the county. It was perfect.

We were touching base one day when I asked her to take on some of the tasks from a project I was working on.

"Absolutely," she said. "But, I'm done with my hours for the week. Is it okay if I start on Monday?"

While I only mumbled in agreement, every cell in my body was screaming. "Out of hours??? This is for the animals! How could she refuse to do anything when it's for the animals?!" I then proceeded to call her a bunch of rather unpleasant names in my head before writing her off as "not caring about the cause."

(Don't worry, I've since admitted this to her. We're still good friends and she won't be hearing about this for the first time while reading my book. In fact, I interviewed her because, obviously, she had boundaries.)

What I didn't realize until a few months after this conversation was that Jamie was establishing those boundaries. Her response to my request was not selfish, self-centered, unhealthy, or cruel in any way. It was the exact opposite: Jamie was standing up for herself in a kind and loving manner. The thing is, not only was I without boundaries, but I also didn't know what they looked like in others.

Imagine this: you were born and grew up in outer space. I know this is not the least bit realistic but stick with me here. You grew up in outer space, a place where gravity does not exist. Then, after living most of your life in this free-floating environment, you touch down on Earth.

Go ahead and tell me you wouldn't have a "What the? Who the? Why the hell am I stuck to the ground?" moment. Of course you would! You've never experienced gravity and, unless you were taught about it as a child, you don't even know it exists. For many of us, boundaries fall into the same category.

In the next chapter, we'll discuss how boundaries are formed. For now, let's discuss what boundaries are and how you can tell if yours are all cattywampus.

Defining Boundaries

In *Facing Codependence*, Pia Mellody defines boundaries as invisible and symbolic "force fields" that have three purposes:

1. To keep people from coming into our space and abusing us;
2. To keep us from going into the space of others and abusing them; and,
3. To give each of us a way to embody our sense of "who we are." (11)

Think about boundaries as property lines. You wouldn't (at least you shouldn't) step onto your neighbor's property and cut down a tree without asking, hang a political sign in their yard, throw a party in their house, or take a big dump on their front lawn. Likewise, you would expect them to follow the same guidelines for your property.

Our bodies, our minds, and our personal effects deserve the same respect. This is where our boundaries come into play. First, let's break them down further so you can see the specific areas where they should exist. Then, we are going to discuss the Goldilocks Principle to determine how much of a fortress you've created.

Six Categories of Boundaries

As you read these, I welcome you to relate them to your own upbringing and life. I know I did. When I first read about the different types of boundaries, it was like a morbid checklist of my own life. I thought about each type of boundary and was easily able to identify a boundary violation I'd experienced.

The six categories of boundaries are Material, Emotional, Mental, Physical, Sexual, and Time. Let's take a closer look.

Material
You have stuff: clothing, a vehicle, a home, food, and toiletries. When healthy boundaries are present, the people in your life know whether or not they can borrow your things and how to treat them. They know whether they must take their shoes off when they enter your home. If you leave leftovers in the fridge, they know whether they are up for grabs or if they shouldn't even think of eating them without speaking to you first. Healthy material boundaries involve teaching people how they may interact with the physical items you "own."

My mom and I moved in with my grandparents when she and my father separated. They had converted the garage and rec room into an apartment years before when my great-grandmother needed a place to live, and we took over that space. It was a first-floor apartment with two entrances. One allowed you to directly enter the apartment from a path beside the driveway. The other door was at the base of the stairs and allowed you to enter the apartment from the rest of the house.

One day, I must've been about eleven or twelve, I was sitting on the couch watching television when my grandmother came downstairs, entered the apartment, and went directly into the bathroom without saying a word. Since most of her "intrusions" were angry and filled with screaming about something or other I'd done "wrong," I considered myself lucky for a few minutes. At least I wasn't being verbally attacked.

I stared on in curiosity before finally walking over and poking my head into the bathroom, "Did you need something?" I asked right before I noticed she was using my stick deodorant.

"No," she responded and slathered on another layer.

"Why are you using my deodorant?"

"Because I can," she said. When she was finished, she went back upstairs without another word.

As a preteen, I was disgusted (okay, I still am today), but I didn't know what was going on, and I certainly didn't have the inner strength to stand up and say, "Please stop using my deodorant. I'd appreciate it if you'd ask me in the future before using my personal possessions." I knew something was wrong, but I didn't have the slightest idea what.

As an adult, I can look back on that and say, "ewww," but also realize that what occurred was a material boundary violation. I didn't know *what* was wrong but I sure as hell knew *something* was wrong.

There's another aspect of material boundaries that may be a little bit less obvious. Your finances actually fall under this category, as well. How do you choose to spend your money? Do you lend it to others and, if so, what requirements are there attached to it? Do you spend more than you have and borrow from others on a consistent basis just to pay bills?

When I look back at my life, I have gotten into debt exactly twice. Neither one of them has been to pay for my own stuff. The most notable was during my first (I like to think of it as my "practice") marriage. My ex-husband had the financial intelligence of a grape. He could not comprehend that if you didn't make money, you didn't have money, or that you couldn't spend more money than you made. Being incredibly financially responsible, I knew this... but I ignored it to make him happy. There was a six-month period when I was out of work and he was only bringing home about $10 an hour. Between the tattoo he "just had to have," the Playstation games that he "couldn't live without," the new phone that was "completely necessary," and all the other irrelevant possessions he insisted on, I wracked up a credit card bill over $10k. It was the only time in my life my credit card payment was more than I could pay in full and I had to carry a balance. I may have had a healthy financial boundary when it came to my own spending but, add another person into the mix, and my boundaries went the way of the dodo bird.

Emotional
My next statement may come as a shock, but I need you to hang in there. You are not responsible for anyone else's feelings, and they are not responsible for yours. Go ahead, read that again. I can wait.

I may be making a sweeping generalization here, but we live in a culture of "he made me mad" or "she hurt my feelings." While anyone can say something insensitive, offensive, or downright toxic, you (and you alone) are responsible for how you interpret it and allow it to affect your emotional state and well-being.

Let's take something as simple as driving a car. There you are minding your own business in the middle lane. You're traveling at a reasonable speed, keeping up with the flow of traffic, when a car flies up behind you and then cuts around you aggressively. You jerk the wheel to the right to avoid an accident and then dispense with a colorful array of swear words and gestures.

Did that other driver make you swerve... yes. Did they make you angry? Nope. You did that all on your own. That driver doesn't have any power over your emotions. They just provided a trigger that set you off. You could have felt amused by their poor driving and began to laugh. You could have felt sad and begun to cry. How you chose to emotionally respond was entirely your choice.

That's rough to hear, isn't it?

Healthy boundaries protect you from allowing others to tell you how you should or shouldn't feel and invalidating the feelings you do have.

To this day, my mom talks about how cute I was when I was little... I mean, I was seriously adorable, but she's talking about one specific behavior: I used to ask her on a daily basis, "Are you happy at me?"

While she thought this was the cutest thing ever, I now realize that it was a major warning flag regarding disordered emotional boundaries. I thought I was responsible for her happiness. If I was responsible for her happiness, guess what else I was taking responsibility for? Oh yeah, her disappointment, anger, unhappiness, anxiety... all the things. In a future chapter, we're going to get into Codependency and how that plays out in regard to boundaries. Spoiler alert: once again, "dumpster fire" doesn't do it justice.

Emotional boundaries also help you avoid sharing too much with the people around you. (Trust me, I've got bartender's disease: Complete strangers spill their guts when they meet me.) Healthy boundaries also allow you to keep your mouth shut when you really want to give advice or criticize someone.

Mental

Considering the political and socio-economic climate we've been living in for the past seven or so years, I actually have to laugh about mental boundaries. Terri Cole, author or *Boundary Boss*, defines mental boundaries as:

> You define your thoughts, values, and opinions. In order to have mental boundaries, you must first know what you believe. Having healthy mental boundaries means that you can listen to others with an open mind, even if you disagree, while

holding on to your core beliefs. Someone making demands instead of requests, disparaging your beliefs, or disrespecting your *no* in an effort to get their way, are examples of mental boundary violations. (35)

I have one word… Facebook. I don't know about you, but I've seen nothing BUT mental boundary violations on social media as of late.

Physical
Your body is your temple. It is your most basic physical boundary and you (should) have full control over who touches you and in what way. Being grabbed, hit, or barged in on all constitute physical boundary violations. And oh yeah… I've got a doozy of an example for you on this one.

There's an old wives tale in the Jewish culture that when a girl gets her first period, the blood drains out of her face. A family member often pats the girl's cheeks to bring the color back in.

My grandmother had a unique definition of "pat." While I wasn't a late bloomer per se, I felt like I waited FOREVER to start my period. When it finally happened, I excitedly announced to my mom, through a closed bathroom door, that I was now a woman. Elated, she ran up the stairs to tell my grandmother. Just minutes later, my grandmother busted through the door and slapped me so hard I actually fell off the toilet.

No matter how old you are, you get to tell people how they can and cannot touch you.

Sexual
Building off of physical boundaries, you have the right to engage in sexual contact (or not!) You get to decide with whom, when, where, and to what degree. Even if you've been with someone multiple times before (and yes, even if you're in a relationship with them), you get to decide when and where. Of course, the other person factors in as well. You must *agree* and both must give consent.

If you've ever done the online dating thing or met potential suitors the old-fashioned way, you've probably encountered a sexual boundary violation or twelve. A few years ago, I went out to lunch with a retired police sergeant. By the time our meals arrived, it was pretty obvious (to me, at least) that I wasn't sitting across from my future husband. After we ate, he walked me to my car and proceeded to pin me to my car with a rather unpleasant, and entirely unwelcome, kiss. I'm not the physically strongest human out there and he had at least a foot on me and probably about 100 pounds. When he came up for air, I squeezed out of the situation and jumped quickly into my car. Could things have been worse? Absolutely? Was it a major freaking boundary violation that didn't fully register until right now? Yup.

Time

I left this one for last because it's probably the one that inspired me to write this book. Time boundaries refer to how you spend your time. Do you work constantly, are you ALWAYS there for your friends, family, boss, fellow PTA members, etc.? Do you spend any time engaging in self-care? Do you fill every moment of your schedule and find yourself exhausted, depleted, and depressed at the end of the day?

There are thousands of books, classes, and systems on time management. The art of fitting it all in and being as productive as possible is quite marketable and incredibly desirable. It's also absurd.

Throughout your day, you will be presented with many "opportunities." While some will move you closer to your life's vision, most of them are actually time sucks in disguise. Being able to identify what you truly want to do, and differentiate that from what you feel compelled to do out of fear of disappointing someone, is the true art. We'll discuss this in greater depth later on and I'll share when I learned this lesson. Spoiler alert: this WAS NOT a dumpster fire! See, we can learn boundaries!

40

Before we jump into the types of boundaries that may apply to these areas, really impactful memes have been showing up in my social media feeds. I wish I could give credit to the original author of this one but there was no attribution:

"I didn't say no because I am busy. I said no because I don't want to be busy."

The Goldilocks Principle
I took a writing class when I first moved to Las Vegas after my divorce. The professor insisted that we could learn everything we need to know about stories from *Goldilocks and the Three Bears*. Do you remember that story? Little girl wanders through the woods until she finds a house. The house's occupants (a family of bears) stepped out for a bit so she makes herself at home.

Well, it turns out, my professor was right about the elements of Story. What he didn't know at the time was that you can also learn everything you need to know about boundaries from our growly friends and a very intrusive little girl.

The Goldilocks Principle states that everyone *has* boundaries… but that doesn't mean they are healthy. I promise this will make sense in just a moment.

Let's start off by saying that Goldilocks needed some major boundary training. Who just breaks into a home in the middle of the woods and starts laying all over their furniture and eating their food? Not cool, Goldilocks. Not cool.

Now let's switch gears. Let's take their beds for example. Goldilocks tried out three beds. The first was too hard, the second too soft. But, the third was juuuust right!

Hop back over to boundary world. The bed that was too hard is called a Rigid boundary. When you have rigid boundaries, you avoid connections with other people. You're afraid to ask for help, avoid close relationships, isolate, and are perceived as unavailable or inflexible by those around you. While you may feel "safe" by avoiding connection, you are also missing out on life.

Moving on to the bed that was too soft. These are Porous or Permeable boundaries and if you are a recovering people-pleaser, you're most likely rocking porous boundaries. You say yes when you want to say no. You overshare personal details before the relationship warrants it. You spend too much of your life trying to fix other people's problems, and you put up with shit that you shouldn't put up with. Porous boundaries cause anger, resentment, and thoughts of driving into oncoming traffic.

Finally, we get to the bed that's juuuust right. Welcome to healthy or flexible boundaries. It's the best of both worlds. You say yes when you want to say yes and no when you want to say no. You share intimate details of your life with the right people at appropriate times. You're happy to ask for help when you need it and provide help when it's asked of you (and not before!). This, my friends, is the Unicorn Zone and we are headed there shortly. First, we're going to take a look at how disordered boundaries *may* show up in your life.

Note: Just because you have Porous boundaries in one situation, doesn't mean you'll have them in every situation. Don't be surprised if you find yourself reacting differently to different people in different areas of your life. That's perfectly normal. Our goal is to get you to the Unicorn Zone with all of your relationships and interactions.

Back To You

Get your fancy (or makeshift) journal ready because we've got work to do!

Referring back to the different categories of boundaries: Material, Emotional, Mental, Physical, Sexual, and Time:

1. In what areas do you find it difficult to create and maintain your boundaries?
2. Are there specific instances you can think of?
3. In general would you say your boundaries are porous, rigid, or juuuust right?

Note: If you haven't already visited www.YouHadMeAtNo.com, pop over there for downloadable worksheets and helpful graphics.

Chapter 3:

Disordered Boundaries

The irony of disordered boundaries is just how easy they are to identify in others. Have you ever seen the movie *Love Actually*? There are several storylines at play, however, Laura Linney's character has been crushing hard on a coworker for years. While she's normally calm and eloquent, when he enters the room, she gets flustered and babbles. We've all been there.

With the encouragement of her boss (we won't discuss whether or not that's appropriate), she speaks to her crush and accepts a date invitation. They end up in her bedroom, clothes flying left and right, and the audience living vicariously as she's gearing up to get a piece.

Until her phone rings.

Her brother, suffering from schizophrenia, lives in a facility. He calls her all day and all night long to voice his delusions. Without their parents alive, Laura Linney takes his call. Every. Single. Time... including the moment when she's going to get everything she's ever wanted. She slides off the bed to take the call and reassure her brother that she's always there for him. Meanwhile, the audience is throwing popcorn at the screen and screaming "What are you doing? Get back in bed! That guy is hot!"

Okay, maybe not the whole audience, but I bet you can relate. It's so damn easy to see when someone else is screwing up a boundary. So easy. Why can't we see it when it's our own life?

Symptoms of Disordered Boundaries

Here are some of the behaviors you may have experienced if you have disordered boundaries.

A. **People-pleasing**—Oh yeah. This is one of the biggest. Do you say yes when you really don't want to do something just because you don't want to upset the people around you? Things such as:

- Going to events you don't want to go to. Can we be honest? Sometimes staying home feels awesome. Snuggling up with your pet of choice, not worrying if your tummy is sucked in, and binge-watching Netflix can be just what the doctor ordered. Unfortunately, if you've got disordered boundaries, you may feel obliged to accept every invitation.

- Doing things you don't want to do. This can include projects at work that you don't have the bandwidth for or taking your cousin to the airport at 3 am because she'd "rather not wait for an Uber." After all, if you don't do something, who else will?

Want to hear something ridiculous? I took seven years of French in middle school and high school. Go ahead, ask if I wanted to take French… I did not. I signed up for Spanish (you know, a *useful* second language for people living in this country). But when I found out that French class might be canceled because it didn't have enough people, I felt bad and switched classes. Yup, I took seven years of a language I have not used once just because I felt bad for the people who *wanted* to take it.

- Taking on more than your responsibility at work (or at home). Do you think if you do other people's work, you'll make friends or catch the eye of your boss? Nope. You'll

47

just have a lot of coworkers who know they don't have to do their own work because you'll do it for them. And your boss is probably thinking (if they even know this is happening) that you don't have enough on your plate and should be their go-to to get things done within stupid timeframes.

- Saying yes to projects you don't have time or bandwidth for. This could be people-pleasing, being afraid of being called "selfish," or it could be a need to prove yourself. We'll get into this more in a bit.

B. **Not having a strong sense of identity**—Do you actually know who *you* are? Or have you spent so much time ignoring your own wants, needs, and preferences? This can show up as:

- Not knowing what your taste is. This realization hit me about 10 years ago. I was about to move into my first home all by myself. Up until that point, I'd gone from living with my mom to a friend to my future ex-husband to my dad and stepmom. At 32, I was moving into a rental and I had full control over the furniture, the decor, and the "vibe" I wanted to go for. Sounds amazing right? Totally something to look forward to.

Nope. I was walking down the aisles at Cost Plus World Market (it's a funky housewares shop in case you don't have it nearby). I stepped into the candle aisle and was instantly overwhelmed by the choices. Candles of every shape, size, and color seemed to be closing in on me. And that's when it hit me… I had absolutely no idea what my favorite color was. I had spent the first three decades of my life allowing other people's tastes to become mine.

I'm not sure I'm the first person to ever cry in that store, but I definitely cried the hardest. After dehydrating for a few minutes, I grabbed a tan candle off the shelf and ran towards the register. Tan. The color of nothing.

- Not asking for what you need (or knowing what you need). I saw a therapist last year for a short period of time while I was going through the really hard part of the rescue fiasco. We were in session one day and she asked me the hardest question of my life:

"What do you need?"

Umm... what's that now? I stared at her, unblinking, like a deer in headlights. No one had ever asked me that question and I didn't have the slightest idea how to answer it. She had me write out a list with six categories:

> ➤ Physical Needs
> ➤ Emotional
> ➤ Social/Relationship
> ➤ Spiritual
> ➤ Financial
> ➤ Fun

Can I tell you, this was one of the most difficult exercises I've ever done. It took me two weeks to get it back to her, and then we moved on to the next questions:

> ➤ Do I have this now?
> ➤ Where is it coming from?
> ➤ Do I need to work on it?

If your head just exploded a bit, I'm sorry. But you do need to know that you: a) have needs, and b) deserve to have those needs met.

- Afraid to express your opinion. I've got a friend who hates Italian food. Of course, I just recently found this out. For years, she'd silently endure pasta every time we went out. Why? Because she didn't want to be difficult. If you're afraid to express your opinion, you may think, "Who am I to disagree?" Whether it's at work, with family, or playing a game of Monopoly in a beautiful beach house, you may not feel that you can speak your mind openly.

- Afraid of conflict. Turns out, this is a hallmark of Highly Sensitive People (we're getting to that soon). Growing up, there were no "conversations" in my childhood, only heated arguments. I learned that disagreements ruined relationships... so, I avoided them at all costs. My fiance, Tom, loves heated discussions and I get visibly upset when we're out to dinner and he starts disagreeing with our friends. He's not doing anything wrong. It's 100% my issues coming through.

C. Not taking care of yourself—

- Being constantly overwhelmed. If you're constantly overwhelmed, there's a good chance you're doing too much for too many people.

- No time for self-care. When was the last time you took an afternoon (or gasp, an entire day) to yourself? When was the last time you turned off your phone and focused on giving yourself a facial, a pedicure, or a good night's sleep? The only time you should be completely sleep deprived because you've put someone else's needs above your own is if you've got a newborn at home. Then, it's acceptable not to shower for a few days and to be walking around so tired that you fall asleep standing… for a little while.

    In an article titled, "Learning to Hear the Voice of Self-Care", Rebecca Pacheco says, "Making time for meaningful connections is self-care. Communicating healthy boundaries with people who intrude on our peace is self-care. Have you ever graciously—without waffling or worrying—indicated that you can no longer tolerate the bull from someone? It's like being given a set of wings."

Disordered boundaries and people-pleasing can show up in a number of different ways. Hopefully, this list has sparked your brain and you can now see a few ways in which you've made other people the most important person in your life.

In *The Devil Wears Prada*, Anne Hathway's character *can't* stop answering her phone when her boss, Meryl Streep calls no matter when or how often she calls. In a conversation with her boyfriend, Anne Hathway apologizes for answering it *again* when they're together. "I have to," she mouths.

He says, "You feel like you don't have a choice. You always have one—you just don't like it."

I promise you, you have a choice.

In the next chapter, we're going to discuss where boundaries come from. But first...

Back to You

Using the worksheets provided in the download (or you can make up your own), do the What Do You Need exercise utilizing all six categories:

- ➢ Physical Needs
- ➢ Emotional
- ➢ Social/Relationship
- ➢ Spiritual
- ➢ Financial
- ➢ Fun

(I know, this can be rough. Take all the time you need.)

Chapter 4:

Where Do Boundaries Come From?

When I was three years old, my mom packed up our things and moved me out of the apartment where we lived with my dad and into my grandparents' house. I was too young to remember living with both parents (though I've been told the screaming was plentiful). However, I have many memories of living with my grandparents… and every day was like World War III.

The environment was explosive and every moment of my life was spent tiptoeing between landmines. I did everything in my power not to set them off. The slightest disagreement would cause an eruption, the presence of which would be felt for days if not weeks. Speaking my mind or sharing my opinion was unheard of. It caused nothing but problems for me and for my mom, who would get the brunt of my grandmother's anger.

The statement, "Children should be seen and not heard" was drilled into my brain and I learned that if I just stay quiet, if I just pretend I don't have needs or opinions, I can "control" the outside world. My childhood goal became nothing more than keeping the peace.

Not that I'm trying to blame parents here, but you may have guessed it… beliefs often get rooted in our unconscious during childhood. They are generally passed down from one generation to the next until someone finally does the work to challenge them. The bad news is, if your family is like most, this hasn't been done yet. The good news is that means you get to do something awesome for future generations! These beliefs then become the basis for our boundary prowess (or lack thereof).

Sometimes we even learn how to have them, or not have them, through the books we were read as kids.

While I was writing this book, a post started to circulate on Facebook. Someone had rewritten *The Giving Tree*, the beloved book about a boy and his best friend (a tree) by Shel Silverstein, so EVERYONE in it had a happy ending. If you remember that story, the tree provided a place to climb, shade, and snacks for his human friend—all things that didn't harm the tree. The act of "giving" to his friend brought the tree joy. However, as the boy got older, he stopped spending time with the tree and only went to visit her when he needed something—like a house or a boat. Though giving up her branches and her trunk would ultimately destroy the tree, she did so anyway, because giving made her happy.

Well, screenwriter Topher Payne set his sights on this book. With his "Topher Fixed It" parody alternate endings to beloved but problematic children's literature, he gave the tree some boundaries and showed us that giving can still be wonderful, but when you have boundaries, everyone wins.

In this new version, when "boy" is all grown up, he goes to the tree and tells her that he wants a house, the tree responds with:

> Okay, hold up. This is already getting out of hand. Look, I was fine with giving you the apples to help you get on your feet. They'll grow back next season anyway. But no, I'm not giving you a *house.* You know, I've seen boys like you pull this nonsense with other trees in the forest. First, it's the apples, then the branches, then the trunk, and before you know it that mighty beautiful tree is just a sad little stump. Well, look here, Boy, I love you like family, *but I am not going down like that.*

I'll put a link to the updated book in the resources section. Just know that the tree shows "boy" how selfish he's been and "boy" changes his ways.

"Setting healthy boundaries is a very important part of giving. It assures you'll always have something left to give." - Topher Payne

Thank you, Topher. The world needed this.

We're going to delve into beliefs more in a future chapter (and discuss how to bust them), but for now, let's discuss the three ways beliefs get locked in:

1. You are told something over and over again.
2. You experience emotional intensity paired with thought (your fear-based emotions are activated).
3. You internalize unspoken messages.

The first way is through repetition. If you hear the same thing again and again during your formative years, the information becomes a belief. Now, this isn't to say that it can't happen when we reach adulthood, however, as children, we don't have any filter from the outside world. If we hear something, we take it in as gospel. As adults, at least there's a chance we might respond with, "That's bullshit," and toss it in the discard pile.

Back to those childhood messages. I've always been very "leggy." I'm only 5'4", but if my torso matched my legs, I'd probably be close to 5'7". As a child, my family thought it was cute to call me Olive Oyl (a cartoon character who was **not** known for her strong, shapely legs). They didn't mean anything by it. In fact, since all of them have battled excess weight their entire lives, they probably thought it was a compliment.

I didn't take it that way. Hearing it over and over again, I developed beliefs about my body. "I'm not pretty." "I'll never be strong." "I have string bean legs, and there's nothing I can do about it."

It doesn't seem to matter how much my fiance (or complete strangers) compliment my legs, I'm still battling this internal belief.

So how do beliefs get locked in? Repetition, for sure. However, things don't have to be said time and time again to become a belief. The second way beliefs get locked in is through emotional intensity paired with thought.

For example, if as a child you experienced a traumatic incident... say you were playing at a safe distance from a campfire on a family camping trip. Your brother, always the troublemaker, decided to throw lighter fluid into the fire. When the fluid hit the flames, they roared up to twice the size and, though there was a good six feet between you and the campfire, the flames hit you, burning your arm.

Your child mind could make all sorts of meaning from this. Perhaps the world isn't a safe place. Maybe your brother is evil, and you can't have a relationship with him. Or, maybe your parents don't love you, and you aren't worthwhile. This fire incident only happened once, but thanks to the provocation of a fear-based emotional state, that experience, and any beliefs that may have stemmed from it, are locked in there real good.

Finally, things don't actually have to be *said* in order to become beliefs. As a child, boundaries are gifted to you. If your parents or caretakers don't supply them, you don't know they exist, that you deserve them, or that you can demand them.

In *Set Boundaries, Find Peace*, Nedra Glover Tawwab talks about how children see how their parents respond to being told no. If parents don't respond well, the child will internalize this and believe they can't say no. Even a parent's nonverbal reaction will communicate to the child that no is acceptable or unacceptable.

Despite what was going on at home, as a child, I was a friendly, outgoing, loquacious kid. I smiled at people in supermarkets and loved to engage in conversations (whether they made sense or not). I had a slight challenge pronouncing my "s" as a child, but my mom worked with me for months to clear that up. (I must've said, "The sneaky snake snuck past the snail and snatched up his snack" about 1,000 times).

One day, my daycare brought in a speech pathologist to evaluate all the kids (all sorts of not okay without parents' approval, but that's beside the point). My mom received a report a few days later that I was having trouble speaking in full sentences. At first, she wondered if my "s" issue had returned, but then she inquired further. The pathologist said that I couldn't speak. She was concerned that my verbal skills were not within range for my age.

Well, it wasn't that I *couldn't* speak, it was that I *wouldn't* speak... to *her*. Maybe she said something to me early on that pissed me off. Maybe, like an animal, I sensed evil and chose not to engage. Either way, I wouldn't give her a peep, and she chose to take that as a complete inability to communicate on my part. When she explained her concern to my mom, my mom responded, "No, she speaks just fine. She just doesn't like you."

My mom respected my boundary in this case and allowed me to assert my preferences. Not every child is so lucky.

Think about how often a young child is brought to a family get-together. "Go ahead, give me a hug," says Aunt Dolly.

Only the kid doesn't want to hug Aunt Dolly. Aunt Dolly gives disgusting wet kisses and smells like moth balls and stale cigarettes. The child refuses, hiding behind his mom. At this point, mom has a few options:

- Push the kid out from behind her and force him to hug Aunt Stinky.
- Embarrass the child and create shame by saying something like, "Don't be rude. It's not nice to say no when someone wants a hug."
- Allow the kid to assert his preference and establish a boundary around who he does and doesn't show physical affection to.

Obviously, the first two options are going to create disordered boundaries and make it difficult for the child to voice his opinions and set healthy boundaries later in life. He will grow up believing that his preferences are unimportant and he doesn't have the right to set boundaries.

The third option is juuuust right.
Parents, while you work through your own boundary journey, please understand that you have the power, and more importantly, the responsibility, to create healthy boundaries for your children.

One more note about childhood before we move on. You may look back at your childhood now and think, "I didn't actually have it that bad. I'm just being silly."

No, you're not. Just because your childhood problems don't seem traumatic now, doesn't mean they weren't traumatic to a child's psyche.

Back to You

It's journal time! Think back to your childhood (and I'm sorry if this is painful).

1. Do you remember any situations that made you feel uncomfortable or like you needed to say no or stand up for yourself?
2. How did your parents respond to you (or others) saying no?
3. Did they verbally or nonverbally communicate displeasure?
4. Did you internalize any messages about whether or not you had the right or the ability to say no?

I know that doing the inner work can sometimes suck. If this is bringing up some ugly shit, make sure you do something nice for yourself (take a bath, take a walk, watch some puppy videos on TikTok) before you try to dive back into your regularly scheduled activities. And if I haven't mentioned it enough yet, if really dark feelings are coming up, you may want to find a professional to speak to. You can reach out to your insurance company to see who is covered, or use a website like findatherapist.com to find someone in your area.

Chapter 5:

The Codependency Correlation

Imagine playing a game of chess in your head. Before every move you make, before every word you utter, before every decision you make, you're thinking about how it will impact other people. If you fall under the categories of codependent, empathic, enmeshed, or highly sensitive, there's a good chance you play that game of chess every moment of every single day.

Don't worry if any of these terms are new to you, we're going to be diving into them one at a time. Now before we start, I want to preface it this way: this chapter is not meant to give you a diagnosis and, therefore, an excuse for having poor boundaries. I believe that no matter what you've been through in your life and what sort of personality characteristics you developed because of it, you can have healthy boundaries. The only reason I've included this chapter is to better help you understand where you are right now and how you can use these "classifications" to your benefit.

Codependency

Let's start out with Codependency since it's kind of the grand poobah from which all of the other characteristics trickle down.

Codependency has many definitions. When someone has an unhealthy attachment to a specific person; when they lose their sense of independence and feel the need to tend to someone else's problems before their own; and when they have an imbalanced relationship and enable someone else's self-destructive behavior—this is all considered codependent. However, what I think describes this condition to a T is, "excessive emotional or psychological reliance on a partner, typically one who requires support on account of an illness or addiction."

Let's unpack that one, shall we? If you were just reliant on someone else to have your needs met, you would be considered "dependent." Codependency is kind of a mind fuck because you NEED the other person to NEED you. Let that sink in for a moment. You derive your worth, your value, from what you do for someone else. This most commonly shows up in families with alcoholism or other forms of addiction. But don't worry, if there was mental illness present in your family... that can cause codependency too!

I was basically raised to take care of others. If I'm not helping someone physically, financially, emotionally, or mentally, well… I don't really know what I'm doing here. And, when people don't take my "advice," let's just say I'm not very pleasant to be around. Go ahead, ask my parents… or Tom.

My first marriage was the perfect example of a codependent, all grown-up, bringing her dysfunction to a romantic relationship. Don't get me wrong, I didn't *cause* the dynamic with my ex, but I certainly *chose* him based on it. When we met, he was in debt. A lot of debt. Further, even after we moved in together, he'd head to his mom's house after work to play video games and have her make him a snack. (I know, so many red flags.) The best part? He was a victim. Everything happened *to him*. He wasn't responsible for any of his actions or the fallout they had. In case you're wondering, no, this didn't stop as soon as we got married, and yes, it got a whole lot worse.

Sure, I could've seen those red flags and run the other way, screaming, Mach 5 with my hair on fire. Instead, I saw him as a project. I could take care of him. I could fix him!

He wasn't a well-functioning adult. But luckily for me, my internal perceived value only went up the more I did for him. Spoiler alert… dumpster fire.

Take a look at your life. Did you grow up in a household filled with addiction or mental illness? Were you trained to care for others? Did you unconsciously or even consciously search for "projects" to fulfill your relationship needs? No shame if you did. This is about learning. If you're just hearing about codependency for the first time, I highly suggest reading *Codependent No More* by Melody Beattie and *Facing Codependence* by Pia Mellody. There's A LOT to unpack regarding this condition and chances are it's trickled into every area of your life.

For now, we're going to head back into the world of boundaries. If you're codependent, you may have problems (according to Pia Mellody):

- Experiencing appropriate levels of self-esteem;
- Setting functional boundaries;
- Owning and expressing your own reality;
- Taking care of your adult needs and wants; and/or
- Experiencing and expressing your reality moderately.

Take a look at number two right there—yup, codependency can mess with setting functional boundaries. Makes sense though. If you derive your value from what you do for others and you need them to need you, when it comes to taking on a project or responsibility, you'll be making a decision while looking through this filter. Saying yes may not meet *your* needs, further *your* goals, or make *you* truly happy… but it will certainly feed your belief that you must take care of others before yourself.

Caring *about* people isn't a bad thing. Caring *for* people isn't a bad thing. The problem is when it becomes the center of your identity. One of my mentors, Ford Saeks, says that when he works with his consulting clients, he is "responsible *to* them, not responsible *for* them," and I think this is a great concept to keep in mind.

When you better understand codependency and how it manifests in your life and relationships, you can avoid the pitfalls and instead embrace the fact that you are a caring, nurturing individual. Use it for good.

Enmeshment

Once you're codependent, it's just a hop, skip, and a jump over to enmeshment. Sharon Martin, LCSW, defines this relationship dynamic as: "Family relationships with weak boundaries, lack of emotional separation, and intrusive demands for support or attention that prevent family members from developing a strong and independent sense of self."

Want to picture what that looks like? Have you ever watched *My Big Fat Greek Wedding*? It's the story of a Greek woman who is surrounded by (and often controlled by) her gigantic family. Parents, aunts and uncles, cousins, etc. are *always* there and *always* weighing in on her life. That's enmeshment in the most severe sense of the word. Everyone is up in everyone else's business. If one family member has a problem it becomes *everyone else's* problem. Perhaps you grew up in a household that wasn't quite as bad but still had elements of enmeshment present.

Martin goes on to say,

> You can be there for people without entangling yourself in their feelings, solutions, and outcomes. The most loving thing you can do is listen. The most empowering thing you can do is allow people to work through their own problems. When you find yourself ruminating about someone else's issues, stop and remind yourself that the issues aren't yours. Tune into your feelings and why you might be stuck on someone else's problems. Enmeshment is a distraction from real ways that we can help others and be there for them. You have never helped anyone by worrying about them and thinking endlessly about their problems.

Interesting because if you're like me, you grew to believe that if you weren't absolutely inconsolable over a relative's or friend's problems, you obviously didn't care about them. Being in a good mood or in a peaceful state when those around you were hurting kind of made you an asshat. If you didn't try to help them (whether they wanted it or not), you were a self-centered prick.

But wait... if I worry about your problems, doesn't that mean *you* don't have to? Oh, if only it worked that way. Worrying for someone or attempting to solve their problems doesn't actually help anyone. Do you know what does help them? Holding a loving emotional state, keeping a clear head, and being available to provide suggestions or assistance (only if asked!). They still own their problem and ultimately their solution, but you get to live your life and still provide love and support. Everyone wins!

Empathy

If you had asked me last year, I would've told you that I was an empath. After years of walking into rooms, feeling the energetic residue of fights that had occurred... and having to immediately walk out because that energy was crushing, I figured that my being an empath was the only explanation. I'd watched *Charmed* as a teenager and I felt Phoebe's pain (all puns intended). It sucked soaking up other people's emotions. I had my own to deal with, why did I need to take theirs on?

One day, I was in my Inner Matrix class (a meditation program) learning how to control my emotions, and someone asked a question about empaths.

"There's no such thing," the instructor said. "They are just falling prey to mirror neurons."

Mirror neurons, in case this is a new term for you, are a class of neurons that modulate their activity both when an individual executes a specific motor act and when they observe the same or similar act performed by another individual. (National Library of Medicine, 2013). In English, that means that when you see someone react in a certain way, you want to act that way too.

To be honest, I felt a little pissed when he said that. I'm an empath, damn it! Don't take away my specialness! But after I put my hackles down, I realized that he wasn't saying I *couldn't* feel other people's emotions, he was saying that I had the choice of whether or not *I wanted to match them.* Ohhhhhh! That's much better. And yes, it would be lovely to have the choice NOT to take on other people's shit.

Then, I found a meme that changed my life (bet you never heard that before!). It said: "Babe, you're not an 'Empath,' you have PTSD from an unstable household and are sensitive to emotional change as a defense mechanism." Credit goes to Fae from IG because I have no idea how to reference an Instagram meme.

Well, well, well. That makes *perfect* sense! Shit was so crazy in my house that I had to recognize—very quickly—what I was walking into for my own protection. Now, you might be thinking that I have gone off on a tangent, but I promise we went here for a reason.

I don't *not* want to be an empath (or a PTSD-driven super-sensitive person). Frankly, I enjoy being able to pick up on people's moods and cut through their bullshit "I'm okay" statements to really help them deal with their crap. That's what makes me a sensitive, caring, individual. What I DO NOT WANT is to be controlled by other people's moods. I don't want to be going along with my day, happy as a clam, when I run into someone who is struggling with clinical depression… and then suddenly feel like my world is crumbling and there's nothing left to live for. No thank you sir. So that's the part I work on. I embrace what makes me me and I work to change what I don't like and don't want to continue.

Now, let's reel it back into boundaries. When you are empathic or even empathetic and take on other people's feelings as your own, you have NO IDEA what you actually need. If you don't know what you need, you can't ask for it. And if you can't ask for what you need, you can't establish and maintain healthy boundaries. Boom.

Highly Sensitive Person

Usually, when I'm reading personal development books, I'm familiar with the psychological terms. Six years of undergrad and master's psych classes prepare you for a lot.

Which is why I was so surprised when I was reading *Boundary Boss* from Terri Cole and came across the term "Highly Sensitive Person (HSP)." I'd never heard of it, but after reading the description, my interest was piqued. I bought the book of the same name by Elaine N. Aron and dove in.

There's nothing quite like the relief associated with finding something that not only describes you perfectly, but gives you *permission* to be who you are and actually outlines why it's a good thing. Learning I was an HSP explained so many things, like:

- Why loud music and repetitive noises impact me the way they do.
- Why I can't handle caffeine.

- Why I'm only comfortable within a 10-degree temperature window. Let's be honest… five degrees.
- Why I'm able to pick up when other people are uncomfortable and help to make them more comfortable.
- Why if I don't eat every two hours or so, I will figuratively and literally chew someone's face off.
- Why I am VERY expressive when it comes to sadness or being overwhelmed and can cry at the drop of a hat.
- Why after a certain amount of mental stimulation, my nervous system is like, "So long, suckas! I'm out!" and I must retreat into solitude and quiet.

There's a quiz if you suspect you might be an HSP. I'll put the link in the resources section.

Once again, you're probably wondering what this has to do with boundary setting. In *The Highly Sensitive Person*, Aron says,

> Most of us get caught up in demands from others. These may be responsibilities or may be the common ideas of what makes for success—money, prestige, security. Then, there are pressures others can bring to bear on us because we are unwilling to displease anyone.

Many HSPs tell me that a major problem for them is proper boundaries—getting involved in situations that are not really their business or their problem, letting too many people distress them, saying more than they wanted, getting mired in other people's messes, becoming too intimate too fast or with the wrong people. (37)

Does that all sound familiar? Codependency, anyone? Enmeshment? Empathy? Dysfunctional boundaries?

The cool thing is that the world can't survive without us HSP's. When others are charging ahead without a care in the world, we are the ones hanging back and yelling, "Wait a moment... do you really think that's a good idea? Let's talk about this before you pillage the situation." Being sensitive to your own emotions, as well as the needs of others, is a good thing... WITHIN REASON.

Hopefully, you now understand the quadfecta (it's a word; I looked it up) of these personality traits or "dynamics" that can contribute to unhealthy boundaries. Hopefully, you can also see that the characteristics that make them up are actually positive and can make us better partners, friends, parents, children, and humans.

In the next chapter, we're going to discuss what happens when we fail to create or uphold a boundary. For now, it's time to go…

Back to You

Got your journal? Good.

1. Do the concepts of codependency, empathy, enmeshment, or HSP resonate with you?
2. Which ones and in what ways?
3. What behaviors can you trace back to these?

Chapter 6:

Boundary Hangovers

"Twenty years from now, you will be more disappointed by the things you didn't do than by the ones you did do." —Mark Twain

Far be it for me to disagree with Mark Twain, but I think there's another facet to this. Yes, you'll regret the things in life you didn't do… and you'll also regret the things you *did* that you wished you said no to.

That's the thing with people-pleasing. You may be making other people happy, but you're not doing a damn thing for yourself. At least nothing good. In this chapter, we'll discuss what you have probably experienced (or have to look forward to), if you spend your life putting everyone else before you.

The weekend of my first wedding, my future ex-husband and I agreed (because that's what his mom wanted), that since our rehearsal dinner had been completed two nights before the wedding, he would spend the evening before with his mom and sisters, and I would spend it with my family and friends.

You'd think that since just about everyone was staying at a hotel a mile down the road from the wedding venue, we'd all just meet for an early dinner close to the hotel and then get a good night's sleep before the big day.

You'd think that wouldn't you?

My mom had recently moved into a new house more than an hour from the venue. She really wanted to host the dinner at her house. It was a generous thought, but not the most convenient idea for the wedding party.

But I had no boundaries. I had no idea how to (kindly) reject the offer and give everyone, not to mention myself, the opportunity to rest. Instead through gritted teeth, I smiled and said, "Sure, we'll all come to your house."

Picture a caravan of five or so cars driven by angry friends and family who didn't want to spend two hours of their night in a car to eat pizza. It's been 16 years since that dinner and, while I'm sure no one gave it a second thought once the weekend was over, I'm still angry with myself for allowing it to happen.

That's the thing with boundary violations. Even if nothing actually *happens* because of them, there are repercussions that can last for years. (Since I'm preparing for my second wedding as I write this book, it's probably time to let go of that anger.) Allow me to give you another example.

Every year, my friends and I get together in early December to do vision boards. We look forward to this all year long because some years, it's the only time we actually get together. We gather at my friend's apartment across town, have snacks and cocktails, and catch each other up on life happenings while we pour over magazines looking for the perfect pictures to represent our goals for the coming year. It's great to spend time with the girls, and it's just about the only time of the year when I let my *visual* creativity out to play. Plus, I get to set the tone for the coming year and visualize all the amazing things that could happen.

About three years ago, our vision boarding day fell on the same Saturday as a professional organization holiday party I was attending. It was no problem. I left my pup with her grandpawrents so I wouldn't need to rush home for potty breaks or meal time. I'd have plenty of time for the glue holding my "vision" on to dry. Then, I could make it across town and have just enough time to shower and get ready before driving to *another* side of town for the party.

It was around 2 pm when the call came. There was an older, past member of the organization who wanted to attend the party but didn't have a ride.

Could I go pick him up on my way and bring him over? I was the first person the president thought of because I was "always so helpful." (How many times have you heard that in your life?)

He gave me the address and my initial thought was, "Nope. I don't want to leave early from an event I look forward to all year long, to drive across town, take a 30-second shower, and then drive 25 miles out of my way to pick someone up that I've never met." And that would've been great to vocalize. If you've been following along thus far, you can probably imagine that it's NOT what came out of my mouth.

Instead, I meekly said, "Umm, yeah I guess I can do that. But if you could find someone else to, that'd be great." We'll discuss the utter ineffectiveness of that statement in a future chapter. For now, I'll just let you know that my car guest was an EXTREME backseat driver and questioned my every turn.

When we arrived at the party, I was angry—mostly at myself—and let it be known that:

- I was not in a good mood, and,
- I had to be up early in the morning to take an adoptable dog on television and would definitely NOT be taking this man home.

How's that for a fun party guest?

The Inner Effects

So what can happen internally when you do something you didn't want to do?

Seething Resentment
In *Facing Codependence*, the author says the following:

> Resentment is the anger you feel when you think someone has victimized you. It might be called "victim anger." It causes me to cling to a need to have the person hurt or punished to make up for the suffering I think he or she has caused me. The person I resent becomes My Higher Power as I think obsessively about what he or she did to me and how I can get even, all the time recreating the shame-filled, pain-filled episode in my mind. (Mellody, 49)

Ouch. Have you been there? I can think of more situations than I care to admit where I felt resentment towards someone. The crappy part... I had caused it all along.

Did you ever watch the show *How I Met Your Mother*? The main character shares the story of how he met the kids' mom through a series of flashbacks. It's brilliant and worth checking out. There's an episode called "The Final Page - Part 1" where they talk about "pit people." Pit people are the individuals in your life who you believe have wronged you. They are the people that you've been obsessed with getting even with for years. These "pit people" are the individuals that you would toss in a pit á la *Silence of the Lambs* style.

Of course, by the end of the episode, every character realizes that the only one down in that pit is themselves. They've been holding onto resentment for so long, and yet the only one they're punishing, the only one they're angry with, is themselves. When you fail to establish and maintain your boundaries, and agree to do something you don't want to do, you "throw people in the pit," harboring anger and resentment that festers. But, you're the only one in that pit and you're the only one who can get yourself out of it.

Missing Out on the Fun
When I became the ultimate party pooper, roaming around mumbling that I shouldn't have had to play chauffeur, I missed out on actually enjoying an evening with friends and associates. Because of my attitude, I probably also missed out on future invitations.

If you get so focused on what you didn't want to do, you'll completely miss enjoying the thing you actually wanted to do.

Burnout

You've spent so much time doing everything for everyone else, you've over-scheduled yourself to the point of exhaustion. As you saw with my last job, simply building in some self-care wasn't sufficient to battle the burnout I was experiencing. I needed to mentally shut down for several weeks just to calm my nervous system back to the point of functioning.

If you're working too many hours, taking on too many responsibilities in your personal life, or otherwise doing too damn much, you may experience:

- Excessive stress
- Fatigue
- Insomnia
- Sadness, anger, or irritability
- Lowered immune system causing you to get sick often
- Alcohol or substance misuse

And if this goes on for too long without correction, you may see:

- Heart disease
- High blood pressure
- Type 2 diabetes

If you're feeling burnt out, now's a great time to reevaluate your life.

Anger Turned Inward

It can be very easy in boundary situations to label yourself the victim who's being taken advantage of by the world. Eventually, though, you start to realize that none of this happened without your approval (or lack of disapproval). When this happens, your anger turns inward and you begin to blame yourself for where you're at in life. Anger turned inward is depression. And frankly, depression sucks.

Loss of Self-Respect

As the resentment and anger build, and as you look to yourself as the source of your problem, you may begin to lose respect for yourself. You may use terms like "pushover" or say things like, "I just can't say no." This makes it worse the next time you're in a situation where boundaries *should* come into play.

The Outer Effects

Up until now, we've been looking at how disordered boundaries can impact our emotional lives. The frightening truth is that when you do something you don't want to do, you'll likely impact those around you as well.

Half-Ass Your Responsibilities

Ever heard the saying, "Do it just bad enough that they never ask you again?" When we take on more than we can handle, or we take on something we don't actually want to do and then get bogged down in resentment, we have a tendency to do the bare minimum to complete the task. If I'm being honest, today marks the end of my term as chapter president for my networking group. While the members believe I did a good job (and I probably did a decent one), I know that I'm capable of much more. The problem? I never should've agreed to it in the first place. I didn't have the time, the emotional or mental bandwidth, or frankly the desire to serve in this manner. If others didn't notice, I'm just left with a slightly degraded sense of self-worth. If others did notice...

Damage Your Reputation

Warren Buffett once said, "It takes twenty years to build a reputation and five minutes to ruin it. If you think about that, you'll do things differently."

If you do a half-assed job on your work responsibilities, a client's project, or something that matters to a friend or family member, you may not only be impacting your current situation but the future, as well. You may get a reputation as someone who doesn't do a particularly good job or doesn't care about the quality of their work. While your boss may have previously considered you for a promotion, they may now be wondering if you even belong at the company. Existing clients may choose not to work with you in the future and may share their experience with others, bad-mouthing you and costing you business in the long run. If your poorly executed responsibilities relate to an area of your personal life, you could potentially jeopardize relationships by letting down the people you care about.

Explode (at an Inopportune Time)
Have you ever been on the receiving end of a reaction that made you go, "Whoah"?

Maybe you asked to borrow someone's stapler in the office and are met with enraged screaming, spittle flying from their lips as they scream, "No one gets to use my mother-freaking stapler!" Or, perhaps they kept quiet one more time and ended up burning down the building. (Why yes, I did just watch *Office Space*.)

There's a really good chance your request didn't cause that reaction. It was more of the proverbial straw that broke our poor camel friend's back. There's also a good chance that you have given a similar response to someone else. Why? Because you neglected to establish and enforce boundaries, let your feelings of resentment, anger, and frustration fester, and then you unloaded on some poor schmuck at the valet or at the grocery store.

It's not okay, but we've definitely all been there.

Potentially Endanger Yourself

In *Stay Sexy and Don't Get Murdered*, one of the authors shares a story from when she was in her late teens and early twenties. A photographer would stop into the diner where she worked just about every day. They would chat, he would show her his portfolio, and they got friendlier and friendlier. Until one day, he offered to photograph her.

She agreed, thinking they'd be walking around town near the diner, taking photos with the city as the backdrop. He had other ideas. On the day of the shoot, he was waiting in his car to drive her to the outskirts of town. She was uncomfortable, but she didn't want to be rude. She was even more uncomfortable when he told her to take her shirt off. You guessed it… she didn't want to be rude. She said the entire time, she was thinking of all the women who get into situations they know are dangerous and then end up being attacked, raped, or murdered. She escaped the ordeal (relatively) unscathed, but always wished she'd been willing to "be rude" and refuse to do something that made her uncomfortable.

Unfortunately, she's not alone. Women (and probably men, too), often ignore their intuition. They silence that little voice in their gut screaming, "Get out of here! Danger, Will Robinson, danger!" because they're afraid to be perceived as "bitchy," "rude," "nasty," or "unkind." *The Gift of Fear* is filled with examples of women who knew there was a very good chance they were going to be victimized in some way, but chose to be "sweet" instead of protecting themselves. Factor in "authority figure" to the equation and few people will refuse to do things that make them uncomfortable.

Open the Door to Future Boundary Violations
"Give someone an inch and they'll take a mile."

This could easily be rewritten as, "Allow someone to violate your boundaries once, and you can expect many more violations in the future."

Okay, maybe the original quote is more catchy, but mine is SO true.

Let's take a look at two examples, one that just happened recently (and thankfully, with my new unicorn-riding boundary battle call, I knew what to do).

For several years, I organized a large festival for the animal rescue. In early October, approximately 7,000 humans and their dogs, cats, ferrets, birds, snakes, etc. would descend on a local park for a day of family, fur, and fun. I was in charge of the vendors and would work with them for months to make sure they were prepared for the day in every possible way. They paid a fee to be there, but anything they made during that day was theirs to keep.

We'd close out the vendor applications two weeks before, leaving plenty of time to pull permits, create a sitemap, and dole out the power hookups to anyone who needed it. Without fail, there would be at least one vendor each year who showed up three days before the event and *absolutely had to participate*. Like, they'd make it sound like the future of their business and possibly the fate of the world as a whole rested on whether or not they had a table at my event.

I'd make concessions, fitting them into our plan at the last minute and rearranging the entire festival layout to make them happy. "Okay, I will fit you in," I'd say. "Please return the application and your check for the vendor fee by the end of the day."

"Absolutely. Oh hey, I'm going to have to buy extra materials for this event… would you mind giving me a discount on the vendor fee?"

Did you see that coming? I should have expected it, but I didn't.

If you allow someone to take advantage of you once, I promise you, they're not done yet.
Let's take a look at a situation that's damn near "in progress."

Besides writing books and speaking to audiences, I write content for businesses like blogs, newsletters, websites, etc. A few months ago, a client reached out to me looking for blogs. Just weeks earlier, my writing fees were all over the map. However, through working with a business coach, I restructured my services and created packages (and fees) more fitting of my experience.

After a few conversations with this potential client, I put together a beautiful (if I may say so myself) proposal and sent it over. I had a price for two blogs per month, four blogs per month, and eight blogs per month. Obviously, the more content a client wanted, the less would be charged per piece.

This potential client received and reviewed my proposal and then... chose his six blogs per month at a price of his own creation.

I know, I know. I probably should've told him to take a hike. But I was excited to bring on another regular client for a six-month duration, so I agreed. Care to take a guess at what happened next? After one month's worth of content at the agreed-upon rate, I received another request.

Here's the email I received:

> Hi Sheryl.
> CLIENT here. I wanted to ask if you would
> charge (less per article) monthly for four
> -1,000 word articles.
> I need one a week and X bucks per article
> is my budget considering other costs I have
> with Search Engine Optimization. I hope
> that will work. Thanks. CLIENT

Thankfully at this point, my boundary antennae
were up, and I knew there was something rotten in
the State of Denmark. I took some time to think,
consulted my business coach, and then penned the
following email:

> Hi CLIENT,
>
> While I certainly understand and
> appreciate a change in your budget, I'm
> unable to accommodate your request. You
> asked for a discount before we began, and
> I agreed, as you had plans to bring other
> business my way. Six blogs at Y is not a
> package that I offer to clients; however, I
> made a special arrangement for you. This
> brought the price to X per blog (less than

even my largest package). Now you are asking for an even smaller package with an even larger discount.

My prices (as noted in the proposal I sent you) are as follows:

- two blogs per month - X
- four blogs per month - Y
- eight blogs per month - Z

If you are unable to select one of these packages or stick with our original agreement, I'm willing to release you from your six-month contract, effective immediately.

Please let me know what works best for you.

I hit the send button and I did a little dance. I stood up for myself! I established a boundary and stuck with it!

Don't you worry, I won't leave you hanging. He agreed. He chose one of my existing packages. Is it still possible he'll try to haggle? Sure. But, I'm prepared for it and ready to release him as a client at a moment's notice.

When you allow someone to violate your boundary or fail to create a boundary in the first place, there are ripples. Whether you feel them internally or see an impact in the world around you, boundary hangovers are very real.

In the next chapter, we will talk about the unhealthy beliefs keeping us stuck in boundaryless purgatory. But first…

Back to You

Ready to dive deep?

Think back to a time when you failed to set or uphold a boundary.

1. What were the circumstances? Go into detail regarding who, when, and what got in the way.
2. Now, what was the internal and external fallout?

Note: This isn't to make you feel bad about yourself. These things happen. It's to help you identify the particulars so you can avoid a similar situation moving forward.

Chapter 7:

Belief Busting

My birthday was a bit of a shit show this year. About halfway through the day, I declared that it was no longer my birthday. I'd be taking a mulligan later on in the month. And I did.

About two weeks later, my fiance arranged for a bunch of my friends to get together for dinner at a local Mexican restaurant (yes, I totally ended up wearing a sombrero) and see this immersive art experience in Downtown Las Vegas called "Particle Ink." They had me hooked from the moment the show "started" in the parking lot. A sheep puppet popped out of some boxes and told us how the next few hours were going to go.

I may hate Monopoly, but I absolutely LOVE puppets. In fact, I grew up on a steady stream of Jim Henson's *Muppets*, so I'm more than comfortable taking life advice from a stuffed animal with a hand up its butt. Which came in handy (all puns intended) at this show. At one point during the evening, I had the opportunity to have my tarot card read by the aforementioned sheep puppet.

He was spot on.

"Oh, I actually don't like this card. This one talks about all the negative, unhelpful beliefs that we hold onto throughout our lives. Yeah, you gotta get rid of those beliefs. Those aren't Truth. You can do it. Please pay on your way out."

I paid my "fee" (a dance of appreciation) and set out to meet the rest of my birthday crew. The puppet was right. Not only was I holding on to some outdated beliefs that were causing me emotional harm, I was also outlining *this very chapter* on how our beliefs can stand in the way of boundary rockstardom.

We discussed beliefs briefly in a previous chapter, but let's dive in a bit more. Beliefs are subconscious or subcognitive, which means they are stored in an area of our brain that we can't necessarily access. Think about that crawl space in your closet that's only accessible using a ladder and a prayer. You store things up there, but it's so damn inconvenient to get to (I'm talking to you, creepy, rickety, splintery, pull-out ladder) that you don't actually remember what's up there. Well, say that you put an old music box up there for safekeeping. That music box is equally creepy and turns itself on every once in a while playing the magical *Nutcracker*'s "Waltz of the Flowers," every few days. (I promise you, this isn't an Edgar Allan Poe story, and there is no one buried in the wall.)

You may not be directly accessing that music box, but you can sure as hell hear the music. That music is your beliefs. They are really difficult to get to, but they are running on a loop pretty much all the time, and just like that music box that might be driving you to action (**now**, it's going to be an Edgar Allan Poe story), your beliefs are driving your actions and making your decisions for you. Keep that in mind as we continue on.

You've heard the saying and seen the meme, "**No** is a full sentence."

It's not wrong. There's just one problem. If you don't believe that you have the *right* to say no, then that's just a fluffy bullshit platitude. First, we need to give ourselves permission to stand up for ourselves; then, we can start dropping no's around town.

According to Chris Williams, MA, LMFT, founder of Renovari Counseling,

> One of the reasons we find it difficult to set boundaries is that we don't know the purpose of the boundary. A boundary is designed to protect that which is valuable. If a person has lower self-worth or doesn't value themselves, they'll have tremendous challenges with boundaries because they won't know what they are actually protecting. This is especially important when it comes to families. When we are younger,

parents determine our value for us. Part of maturation is owning that for ourselves. We need to own and protect our personal value.

Is it tacky to quote yourself? Well, it's a risk I'm going to take because I was actually talking about this very thing in my first book. In *Surviving to Thriving: How to Overcome Setbacks and Rock Your Life*, I said,

> The way I see it, most of the world's problems are due to a lack of self-esteem. I know, that's a huge sweeping statement and I'm gonna stick to it. In my own life, I can attribute all of my stupid decisions to a lack of self-esteem. If I had believed in myself more, if I had considered myself worthy of setting and maintaining boundaries, if I had the confidence to pursue greatness rather than settling for mediocrity, let's just say life would be a tad different.

And guess what? Low self-worth... is a belief.

Let's take a moment and approach this from an anthropological standpoint. Consider that our ancestors spent their days doing their absolute best not to get eaten. No, I'm not talking about your grandparents (though what do I know about your family tree?). I'm talking about our Cro-Magnon ancestors. We may think we're top of the food

100

chain these days, but when you've got bears and tigers and other large predators sniffing around your campsite at all hours of the day and night, there is one thing that will get you killed faster than teasing a lion on a juice cleanse... being alone.

We are social creatures meant to live in tribes, surrounded by family and friends who can "watch our back" while we sleep and vice versa. If you pissed off your tribe and were cast out on your own, there was a really good chance you'd become dinner for some large, furry beast.

In *The Gift of Fear*, de Becker says,

> Surveys have shown that ranking very close to the fear of death is the fear of public speaking. Why would someone feel profound fear, deep in his or her stomach, about public speaking, which is so far from death? Because it isn't so far from death when we link it. Those who fear public speaking actually fear the loss of identity that attaches to performing badly, and that is firmly rooted in our survival needs. For all social animals, from ants to antelopes, identity is the passcard to inclusion, and inclusion is the key to survival. If a baby loses its identity as the child of its parents, a possible outcome is abandonment. For a human infant, that means death. As adults, without our identity as a member of the tribe

or village, community, or culture, a likely outcome is banishment and death. (342)

While there's a much smaller chance of being eaten these days, that need for security and companionship is wired into us. It may no longer mean imminent death to be ostracized by your peers, but it certainly feels like it.

Why did we go down that road? Because many of our "need to please" behaviors come from a fear of being abandoned. Let's take a closer look at some of the common beliefs that prevent us from standing up for ourselves:

1. If I say no, people will stop liking me.
2. If I don't take on extra work, I will be fired.
3. If I don't give up my one day off to help a friend, they will be disappointed and no longer want to be friends.

Can you see how all of these are rooted in, "I will be abandoned and cast out of the tribe?" It's just a hop, skip, and a jump for our lizard brains to reach, "... and then I'm going to be eaten."

With the fear of becoming dinner off the table (oh yeah, pun intended), we can now ask the question, "What's the actual worst that might happen?" Even though our brain wants to go there, now is the time to avoid catastrophic thinking.

In *Set Boundaries, Find Peace*, the author says, "Even though the worst case is the least likely outcome, when you're anxious, it's exactly what you work hard to avoid. But the true worst-case scenario is avoiding boundaries. Saying no to others always allows you to say yes to yourself or to things you truly want."

She then goes on to identify Nine Potential Reasons Why You Can't Sufficiently Set a Boundary:

1. You fear being mean
2. You fear being rude
3. You're a people pleaser
4. You're anxious about future interactions after a boundary has been set
5. You feel powerless (and not sure that boundaries will help)
6. You get your value from helping others
7. You project your feelings about being told no onto others
8. You have no clue where to start
9. You believe that you can't have boundaries in certain types of relationships (60)

Right now I'm reminded of George Carlin's bit about the Ten Commandments. He lays out each commandment and identifies whether it should be its own commandment (since many overlap) whether it should be a commandment at all (or doesn't deserve to be), until finally, he ends up with

103

just two commandments. Let's do that with our list of potential reasons, shall we? Because really they boil down to four. Hang in there, we're going out of order and I don't want you to get whiplash.

Number eight, not knowing where to start, can get knocked out because you've already started. Further, in the next section, we're going to break it down for you so you know EXACTLY how to establish and uphold your boundaries.

Number seven is about not liking it when someone tells *you* no. Don't assume that because you have dysfunctional boundaries other people do as well. In fact, as we'll discuss in the next chapter, it's fairly easy (even now) to set boundaries with people who, themselves, have healthy boundaries.

Number five, being powerless, sounds to me like worst-case thinking. What if you establish a boundary and it doesn't work? What if you tell someone not to do something and they go ahead and do it anyway? But here's the thing, you are NEVER powerless. You may not be able to control how they react to you and your new boundary, but you can control whether they are in your life. We'll talk about that in Part Three.

Number six is about codependency. When your self-esteem is based on what you do for others, then *not* doing for others could be a real blow to your identity. Wait… did I just say that your identity is in jeopardy... and didn't we just learn that your identity is tied to inclusion within the tribe? That sounds an awful lot like one, two, three, four, and nine. And you know what? Those all boil down to being afraid you're going to get eaten.

I'd been doing belief work for a while when the puppet imparted his wisdom, but I decided to see what thoughts were plaguing others. I began asking friends, "What's a belief that no longer serves you?" I got some doozies.

As I rattle these off, look at them through the lens of, "I don't wanna get eaten!"

- "I have to be perfect."
- "I'm not worthy of love."
- "I'm not doing enough."
- "I must constantly achieve to be worthy of love."
- "Being willing to sacrifice myself for the good of my family makes me a better mom." (She realized it didn't... it just made her tired and cranky.)
- "I have power over other people's emotions and moods."
- "Disagreements end relationships so it's best not to voice opinions."
- "I am not safe or secure. The rug could be ripped out from under me at any time."
- "My self-worth is derived from what I do for others."

Did you notice a pattern? If we haven't been taught that it's our innate right, boundary setting endangers our belonging, therefore, it threatens our sense of safety and security.

When we have a belief, we will do our best to uphold it.

Melissa, one of my Inner Matrix teachers, put it best. "The mind is a great lawyer. It will find evidence to support your beliefs if you look for it."

Your mission (if you choose to accept it) is to bust the beliefs that are no longer serving you.

After I moved to Las Vegas and got through my depression, I worked with a career counselor to find some direction, get my resume in tip-top shape, and learn the best way to get a job. Basically, I wanted someone to sit next to me and pet my head while I applied for jobs I didn't believe I was qualified for while batting the Imposter Syndrome demons. She did the next best thing… she taught me how to do it myself.

The career counselor taught me about the T-Cover Letter. Basically, you draw a line across your paper from left to right, then a line down the center of the page (you know… like a "T"). On the left side goes the qualifications that the job post is looking for. On the right side goes how your experience meets those qualifications. Let's look at a quick example before we apply this to the wonderful world of boundary setting.

"T" Cover Letter

Qualifications	Your Experience
5+ years in a management role	Level 2 Supervisor (7 years), responsible for 30+ employees

Figure 1: T Cover Letter

Get it? Now, what the hell does this have to do with boundaries and beliefs? We just used the T-structure to *prove* why we're right for the job. Now, we're going to use it to *disprove* our unhealthy beliefs.

When you know your worth and your values, and when you bust through those unhealthy beliefs, boundaries become so much easier. Next, we'll talk about why you may already be setting boundaries with some people while struggling with others.

Back To You

Now we get to work. Write down the beliefs that are bouncing around in your mind. Realize that you may have to do some digging. Those little bastards are hiding, and it's going to take some work to get them out. A therapist can help you uncover these beliefs, and you can also do some mindfulness exercises to start the process.

When you feel upset, instead of distracting yourself or attempting to cover up your feelings, lean into them. Chances are that you're experiencing some physical feelings in your body as well. Sit quietly and listen. What are the thoughts that are popping up in your head? (Note: Beliefs are like whack-a-mole at the carnival. Once you smack one down, don't be surprised if another one pops up.)

Grab your journal and create your T on the paper. (You've also got a worksheet in the downloads.) To the left of the vertical line, you're going to write "Belief," and to the right of the vertical line, you'll write "Why It's Bullshit." If you'd prefer not to curse like a sailor, feel free to say, "Why It's False."

Belief Busting

Yucky Belief	Why It's False

Figure 2: Belief Busting

Next, we're going to create another T-chart. We need to replace these old, outdated, yucky beliefs with new, shiny, helpful beliefs. Then, we need to find evidence for them. On the left side, write down "New Belief" and on the right side, "Proof."

Belief Creation

New Belief	Proof

Figure 3: Belief Creating

Think about it this way: when you make decisions based on your beliefs, you are essentially allowing an eight-year-old to drive your car. You wouldn't do that in reality (I hope), so why don't you go ahead and take the keys back.

Chapter 8:

Why Are Boundaries More Difficult With Some People Than With Others

Well, that's the million-dollar question, isn't it? While some people have an issue creating boundaries with anyone and everyone, others will find that their boundary-setting deficiencies are only triggered by *certain* people. If this resonates, this chapter is for you.

Our lives are intertwined with others. There are people that come into our lives for five minutes, others that will be in our lives for five weeks or five months, and some who will grace our existence for five years or five decades. The closer we are to someone, the more important they are to us, and therefore the more difficult it may be to set boundaries with them. The people who will be in your life for years or even decades (your parents, kids, significant otter—not a typo, and your friends) are closer to you and therefore create a bigger impact. Those who will be in your life for a few minutes (the checkout woman at the grocery store or the Amazon driver who drops off your package) are further away with less influence and impact.

| You | Significant Otter | Close Family and Friends | People you know but aren't close with | People you've met once or twice | Strangers |

Figure 4: Impact Based on Relationship

Boundaries and your ability to set them are based on your relationship with the individual and the potential outcome of your decision.

Consider this, if the checkout woman at the grocery store is throwing your food into grocery bags and your eggs are in danger, you'll probably say something. After all, she's violating a material boundary and whether or not you can identify that you know that it's going to be really hard to make breakfast tomorrow morning if this assault on your eggs continues. You *may* say something. But if you don't, it's not because you're afraid of the long-term fallout of advocating for your eggs with a complete stranger. If you don't say something, it's probably because you don't want to be seen as "rude" (which still relates back to not wanting to be ostracized from the tribe and therefore eaten).

Now, let's consider your mother-in-law who has insisted on hosting Thanksgiving again this year, even though she's done it every single year and you just moved into a new house with a state-of-the-art kitchen, and you really want the opportunity to have your turkey shine. You've got a relatively good relationship with your mother-in-law, and heaven knows, it's easier for your husband when the two women in his life play nice.

You want to stand up for yourself. You want to explain that you've been waiting years to throw a Thanksgiving bash and your new home is set up perfectly for entertaining. You want to invite a few friends you can't invite if you go elsewhere. You want to host, damn it! But… what will the fallout be? What's riding on you speaking up for your wants and setting a boundary?

It could change the relationship you have with your mother-in-law. It could make your husband's life more difficult as you "force" him to choose sides. He could choose her. You could end up divorced. You could end up alone. Homeless. With a colony of feral cats as your only family.

How did I do? Did I capture the crazy spiral that we find ourselves in? You know, there's another possibility here. You could talk to your husband and explain why hosting Thanksgiving is important to you. When he understands (and hopefully supports you), you can approach his mom as a unified (but gentle) front and state your case. You never know, she may have been insistent on hosting because she didn't want you to have the added stress after you'd completed a move while still working a 40-hour-a-week job.

It's really easy to death spiral into the worst-case scenario, but it's not always (or usually) the reality.

In *The Assertiveness Guide for Women*, Julie de Azevedo Hanks, Ph.D., LCSW says: "Why is it often scarier to express our feelings, thoughts, needs, and wants to those closest to us? It is because there is a greater risk involved; we have more at stake, and therefore more to lose with our loved ones." (23)

While boundary-setting challenges generally depend on relationships, there's often another level to this. If they were solely based on relationships, then people in the same category (like Close Family and Friends) would inspire the same challenges. For example, your parents are likely on the same ring, therefore you'd be unable to set boundaries with both of them for the very same reason. Not so true.

To uncover the next layer, we need to look at the individual person, their personality, and the emotions they trigger in us.

For one person, we may find it difficult to set boundaries because we don't think they can do something themselves or don't believe they have the resources or support to do something if we don't do it for them. This is likely rooted in codependency.

I was speaking with Chris Williams, MA, LMFT, about this topic and he introduced me to the Drama Triangle or the Karpman Triangle. Are you sitting down? This one is going to blow your freaking mind.

In the Drama Triangle, there are three roles:

1. The Victim/Helpless
2. The Rescuer/Savior
3. The Persecutor/Bully

The Victim depends on others, avoids responsibility, and seeks a rescuer.
The Rescuer is over helpful. They feel responsible for other people's problems and make sacrifices for others while denying their own personal needs.
The Persecutor is critical, rigid, bossy, dominating, driven by anger, and uses guilt to control others.

Makes sense, right? We can see ourselves and the people we know in these roles. Here's where you need to hold onto your underpants... When we find ourselves in Rescuer energy—when we've identified someone who is a "victim," someone who can't do for themselves—if we don't help them, we feel as if we become the persecutor.

Well slap my ass and call me Sally! Are you kidding me? So, we can be moving along, minding our own business when we come upon someone who we perceive to need our help. We can either help them (which has so much other fallout as we've been discussing) or we can let them handle it on their own and believe that we are now doing them just as much harm as whomever (or whatever) got them into that situation in the first place.

Daaaaamn.

For another, we may fear how we will feel if we set a boundary. Now, what I really wanted to say was, "how they will make us feel," but I've done way too much work on my emotions to fall into that trap.

Let me explain. There are people in our lives who will assume that our attempt to set a boundary is an attack on their person. In order to protect themselves, they will shame you. No, they won't just "make you feel" guilty, they will inspire shame. If you're wondering about the difference, Brene Brown has laid it out for us. "Guilt is I did something bad. Shame is *I am* bad."

I haven't seen the movie *Raising Helen* with Kate Hudson in about five years, but I've never forgotten one line. Joan Cusack (the main character's older, wiser sister who is already a mom) goes with Hudson to rescue her "daughter" from a prom night deflowering. When they bust into the motel room, Cusack yells at the boy and says, "You're not a bad person, but you did a very, very bad thing!"

To me, that perfectly captures the difference between guilt and shame. When something happens, do you feel bad about what you did, or do you internalize the feeling and believe that you *are* bad? Even though standing up for yourself and setting boundaries isn't a bad thing, there will be people in your life who treat it as such. You may feel guilty about setting a boundary, but that's not a reason not to do it.

As I've been writing this book, I've been doing more inner work and dissecting every boundary-related experience I've ever had. One more thing occurred to me regarding the individuals who are easier or harder to set boundaries with.

Their boundary-setting abilities.

Sometimes, it's easy to set a boundary with someone because they, themselves, have healthy boundaries. While it may be unconscious knowledge on our part, when we talk to someone who has healthy, successful boundaries in play, we know they will understand. We don't fear they'll excommunicate us from the tribe just because we say no. On the other hand, when dealing with someone who appears to have weak or disordered boundaries, we don't know what their reaction will be if we don't do what they say. This is why it's so important to:

> a) surround yourself with people who have healthy boundaries, and,
> b) respect other people's boundaries.
> (Both of which we will discuss in a future chapter).

There's one more ring of your orbit that we need to touch on here... you. Yup, there you are sitting at the center of your world, doing your damnedest to learn how to set boundaries with others. However, if you don't have boundaries with yourself, if you don't show yourself respect, why would you expect anyone else to?

Boundaries with yourself can look a bunch of different ways. Such as:

- Establishing and maintaining a healthy morning routine so you are ready to face the day with a clear, positive mind.
- Gifting your body with regular physical exercise, whether you go to the gym, walk 10,000 steps each day, or have a morning yoga practice.
- Eating a healthy diet and not "rewarding yourself" with junk.

- Going to bed at a reasonable time each night rather than binge-watching the Home Shopping Network until you can't keep your eyes open and end up late for work the next day.
- Curbing the negative self-talk and not allowing your mind to run amok (amok, amok!)
- Prioritizing self-care and taking time each day to pamper yourself (even if it's just in a small way).
- Budgeting and only spending what you have rather than racking up credit card bills while binge-watching HSN late at night.

Don't worry, if you just let out a loud, "Well shit," you're not alone. We don't often consider the way we treat ourselves to be indicative of how others will treat us. However, standing up and saying, "I'm important!" through our actions, communicates to others that we won't be taking any more shit. We truly do train others how to treat us... but first, we have to train ourselves.

Back to You

We unpacked quite a bit in this short chapter, so we're going to tackle a few exercises here. Don't worry, you've totally got this. Grab your journal and let's play.

1. Create your impact stick figures. (I've created one for you in the downloads) and place the people in your life in the proper position.
2. Select the people in the first two or three positions (closest to you) whom you find it the most difficult to set boundaries with and circle them. Now, we're going to take a look at each of them, one at a time. Why do you think boundary setting is a challenge with this person? Now, don't worry about fixing it. We'll get to that in the next section. For now, we're just identifying who they are and why it's a struggle for us.
3. Last but not least, in what areas are you not setting and respecting your own boundaries?

Part 2:

Learning a
New Language

Chapter 9:

Do You Actually WANT To Do Something

Earlier this year, I was approached by a good friend of mine. She was stepping into the role of President of our local Speakers Association chapter and she wanted me to join the board, and become the President-Elect so I could take over the chapter next year.

I'd served on the board a few years earlier and deep down knew the commitment I'd be making. But I chose to believe her when she said, "Oh it's only about an hour of work each week."

Truthfully, being President always sounds cool. I was looking to get back into professional speaking after a pandemic-induced career switch (I hung up my microphone to work full-time for the animal rescue). And, since I owe damn near everything I've achieved to my networking skills, the opportunity to connect with speakers around the country and have an official "title" while doing it appealed to my inner extrovert and appeased my Imposter Syndrome.

There was just one problem… I couldn't bring myself to say yes. She'd ask me every few days, and I'd always answer with, "Let me talk to Tom," or "I have to take a look at my schedule," or "I promise, I'm thinking about it." The truth was the biggest driver for me considering the volunteer position was not wanting to disappoint my friend.

So when she said, "I need to know by Friday. I have to have the board situated by then," I gave her the yes she wanted. And then the emails started.

I counted between 10 and 15 a day—not including the calendar invites. There were meetings. There were national meetings. There were local meetings. Then, there were meetings to discuss the meetings. All in all, we were looking at about two hours of meetings each week… and that didn't include the work I'd be doing in between.

Don't get me wrong, I love to serve. I think you've already figured that out about me. But, while building a business, planning for a wedding, and taking on more responsibility for my aging parents, the idea of death-by-meeting was not exactly appealing. When a call for help came from a foster dog I'd cared for on and off for years, and I had to drop everything and drive to Colorado the day of our big "board retreat," I began to realize that I'd gotten into something I shouldn't have.

I spoke to a mentor a few days later. "If you don't have the bandwidth to serve your chapter the way you want and the way in which it deserves, you'd be doing everyone a disservice by staying in the role."

Three days later, I was sitting on an airplane with a dead Kindle, taking stock of my life. I never should've said yes to the position—and now I needed to get out. Oh, and I should probably write a book on boundaries.

Throughout this book, we've been discussing why you may be afraid to or feel uncomfortable setting boundaries. With that understanding, it's time to venture into a solution. You don't need to spend the rest of your life doing things you don't want to do, putting other people's needs above your own, or doing things that make you uncomfortable just so you don't upset someone else. It's a new day and, our romping unicorn friend is just a few chapters away.

When I first sat down to figure this out, I began to draft an If/Then chart. It had about 30 different paths you could take and, frankly, it was giving me a headache. If it was too complicated for me (the designer), it was for sure going to be too complicated for anyone else. So I set out to create something a lot easier.

Helloooooo Venn diagram! I call this the Clash Question since you are essentially asking the question, "Should I Yay, or Should I No."

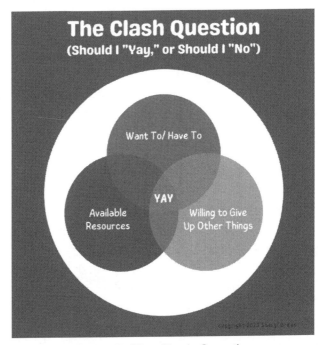

Figure 5: The Clash Question

Now, before you look at it and say, "This doesn't help when I HAVE TO DO everything!" we are going to discuss that.

I know it's an oversimplification of a very in-depth process. Don't worry, we're going to dive into that. I wouldn't leave you hanging.

So, let's break it down:

- Do I want to or have to do something?
- Do I have resources available to carry it out?
- Am I willing to say no to other things in my life?

Want to/Have to

For some, knowing whether they want to do something is pretty straightforward. You're either excited about it and can't imagine *not* doing it, or the thought of doing the thing makes you want to stick pins in your eyes.

I'll give you an example. My friends are really into triathlons and races like the Tough Mudder. They've invited me a few times and, while I love spending time with them and would go along if they suggested something only mildly off putting (ahem Monopoly), there is no part of me, not even a little one, that wants to do a race like that. Running? Only if I'm being chased. Biking? Nope, can't do it. Seriously. It's so frightening to me that I put my nails through the palms of my hands. Swimming? Do I get my own personal lifeguard? My butt is made of lead and I can drown in a kiddy pool. Electrocution? Really... do I need to explain why I'm not into this one? Ice cold plunges? Not even at the spa. The mud doesn't sound too bad, but if I don't have cucumber slices over my eyes during a mud experience, is it even worth doing? This is a definite Hell No for me.

For others (and for me in less clear-cut situations), especially those who have struggled with codependency, enmeshment, or being an HSP, knowing what you want is actually really difficult. Is this something *you* want to do or is it a residue of someone else's desires or goals? Hang in there. In the next chapter, I'm going to share how to listen to your body (it knows… your brain is just getting in the way).

Let's look at a few reasons why you might want to do something:

- It aligns with your goals and will help you get closer to achieving whatever it is you want to achieve.
- It's fun!
- You truly want to help someone out of love not fear.

What about Have To? If you fall into one of the aforementioned categories, you already believe that you *have to* do everything. You don't. I'd venture to say (and remember that 82.35% of statistics are made up) that 60-70% of what you think you have to do, you don't actually have to do.

Ask yourself the following questions:

- Is this life or death? If you don't do the thing, will someone die? Or is this really more of an inconvenience for someone else?
- Will you lose your job/client? When you work for someone else, you do have to do what they say... to a point. If you've been given a wholly unreasonable workload that will cause undue harm to you or make you unable to do any of your work properly or you've been asked to do something that blurs the lines of your integrity, you have every right (and responsibility) to say no. In a future chapter, we'll discuss the Improv method of adding conditions to your "yes" response.
- Am I doing this for someone who cannot take care of themselves and it is my actual responsibility to care of them? (This is no time to tell your three-year-old or your elderly parents that you can't take them to the doctor as promised).

Realize that for the past X-amount of years, you've likely been operating as though everything is a "have to" situation. It's probably not. There's a good chance that what you've been compelled to do, trained others you're willing to do, and believed the world would end if you didn't do... doesn't actually fall under the "have to" classification.

Now that we've clarified the top bubble, let's move to the lower left—Available Resources.

Available Resources

You may *want* to do something. You may *have* to do something. But, *can* you do the thing? Resources fall into four categories: time, financial, emotional, and mental. Sometimes as much as you'd like to do something for yourself or others, you just don't have the means to.

Time

There is no shortage of "opportunities" around us. People offering you volunteer positions, network marketing companies to buy into, parties to go to, charity events to attend, learning opportunities, etc. Some of these opportunities are real. They'll help you either get closer to your goals or have fun.

However, most of these are actually time sucks disguised as opportunities. They look shiny and fun at first glance, but when you dig down, (or say yes and live to regret it), they are like the wolf in *Little Red Riding Hood*, dressed up as grandma but ready to eat you at the drop of a cape. Or, like Dracula… "I've come to suck your time!"

You have a finite amount of time (which we'll discuss in a moment), so use it wisely.

Financial

For some, this is the easiest resource to regulate; for others… no bueno. Things cost money. You may have time to go to a conference and improve your work skills, but can you afford the conference itself? How about the travel costs like air, hotel, transportation, food, etc.? You may totally want to go skydiving with your friends because it speaks to your thrill-seeking side. But skydiving should be expensive (and if it isn't, look elsewhere—this is not the time to bargain shop).

Sometimes, development opportunities can be considered an investment in yourself. Just be careful not to partake in ALL the development opportunities.

Emotional

I'll be honest, I needed some real help on this one. I've always had an "If you need me, I'm here for you" attitude. While that may be honorable, it certainly doesn't take any level of self-care into account. If you can't handle your own emotional shit, how are you expecting to handle other people's?

My therapist said it best: "How full is your cup? Are you in a place to offer support? If you have nothing to give, you can barely be empathetic and it's not useful for anyone."

To summarize: You can't give away what you don't have.

Well, damn. It makes sense. But, boy, is that hard to comprehend when you've spent your life trying to fix everyone else's problems and believing that you actually have control over their emotions.

Check your emotional cup. If there are just undissolved coffee grounds in there or the grime that inevitably sneaks out of the tea bag, you are in no place to take on other people's emotional garbage. If you're in a good place and can be empathetic, caring, and hold space for them, pull up a chair and lend an ear.

Mental
I've never loved the term "bandwidth" (I know, I used it earlier) because it makes us sound like computers and that's just a few inches away from *The Terminator* coming true. But it really does capture the sentiment here. There is such a thing as "too much." There are times in our lives when we've got a huge project to finish; we are in building mode with our business; when we are planning a big event; when we are taking care of a loved one; and when we are dealing with our own medical diagnosis that it's just "too much."

But, the "opportunities" won't stop coming. The demands on our time won't stop coming. We just won't have the bandwidth to deal with them. You can only do so much (sorry, Superwoman, I know you've been told otherwise) and taking on more won't end well.

Willing to Give Up Other Things

In *Four Thousand Weeks*, Oliver Burkeman points out the (sobering) fact that we only have four thousand weeks here on this planet. Some may live longer and some may die sooner, but the average person has four thousand weeks to leave their mark on the world. It's depressing in that it makes you realize that you won't get everything done that you want to do. It's uplifting because you realize that you won't get everything done… so you better choose wisely.

Make no mistake, when you say yes to one thing, you will have to say no to something else. If you agree to work over the weekend because your coworkers have been slacking and your boss expects you to pick up the extra weight, you will have to say no to girl's weekend, your sister's birthday party, your husband's golf tournament, Harvest Festival at your son's school, or just laying on the couch decompressing and watching Netflix with your terrier/chihuahua mix.

Sacrifices will be made.

Before you agree to do something (anything really) really consider whether you are willing to say no to all the other things you'll have to say no to. Going out drinking Friday night may seem like a great way to blow off steam after a difficult week. But are you willing to say no to the 8 am Farmer's Market Saturday morning that you've been looking forward to for weeks?

Before you blurt out "yes" to your friends, family, boss, or that woman on the PTA committee who always makes you feel like you don't do enough, use the Clash Question. If a 'yes' doesn't fall into that sweet spot where Want To/Have To, Available Resources, and Willing to Give Up Other Things meet, you know what you have to do.

And because you should never be too proud to take advice from a Muppet, as the Trash Heap (the wisdom-filled pile of garbage from Fraggle Rock) says, "Yes means yes, and no means no. If it's not a big yes, it's a no-go!"

Back to You

1. What decisions do you need to make right now?
2. What would have been your go-to response before reading this chapter?
3. Now, use the Clash Question diagram, (it's in the downloads at www.YouHadMeAtNo.com) to work through it.

Chapter 10:

When the Answer Is No

You've probably heard the phrase, "Listen to your gut." While sometimes our gut is "talking" out of fear, it really is talking to us. There's this thing called Visceral Afferent Messaging, which is the conduction of messages from our internal organs. When you get that hollow feeling in your stomach or your heart won't stop pounding and there's no physical reason, it's your body trying to get your attention.

In *The Gift of Fear*, Gavin de Becker says,

> What [some] want to dismiss as a coincidence or a gut feeling is in fact a cognitive process, faster than we recognize and far different from the familiar step-by-step thinking we rely on so willingly. We think conscious thought is somehow better, when in fact, intuition is soaring flight compared to the plodding of logic. Nature's greatest accomplishment, the human brain, is never more efficient or invested than when the host is at risk. Then, intuition is catapulted to another level entirely, a height at which it can accurately be called graceful, even miraculous. Intuition is the journey

from A to Z without stopping at any other letter along the way. It's knowing without knowing why. (28)

When I was in college, I was dating a hot mess. I'm not trying to be cruel. He had a whole host of emotional problems and would physically bang his head up against a wall when he didn't get his way. (Side note: I didn't want to date him. I just wanted to be friends. But, he said we couldn't be friends if we didn't go out, so I gave in… dysfunctional boundaries much?)

So, the first few weeks were *okay*. But it wasn't long before I started having heart palpitations. I'd be lying there watching TV or studying and my heart would start pounding out of my chest. I don't think I even knew what an anxiety attack was at that time, so I assumed I was having a heart attack. My mom insisted I see a doctor and the tests began. EKGs, a CT, an X-Ray, and finally, a Holter monitor that I had to wear over Thanksgiving to get a better picture of what was going on with my ticker.

The diagnosis? Nothing. Absolutely nothing abnormal.

So I went to a psychologist. She needed no medical equipment to tell me that I was miserable in my relationship and my body was screaming, "What are you doing!?!? Run!!!!" (And she was a student, no less).

That's the funny thing about our bodies. They know things. Things that our minds and souls aren't quite ready to admit. I'd love to tell you that I went home and broke up with him that very day. But I didn't. I figured I could stick it out for a while and my feelings would change. Long story short: it didn't end well.

I want to share one more example before we dive into what this means for you and your boundaries.

A few months ago, I was having lunch with a friend. She was going through the Weight Watchers program and shared something her group leader told her.

"Apparently, we sigh when we are full. When she told me, my first reaction was, 'Oh, I don't have that.' But then, I was eating a few days later and I sighed!"

She was so excited to share her newfound full-belly indicator that I didn't have the heart to tell her I don't have that. But wouldn't you know it, a few days later, I was eating dinner and I sighed. I do have that!

That sigh is our body's Visceral Afferent Messaging at work. And if we listen to it (and actually stop eating after that sigh), we won't feel like we are about to give birth to taco baby triplets. I'm happy to say that I almost always notice my sigh… and most of *that* time, I actually stop eating. Look at that, boundary education and dieting tips. Aren't you lucky?!

Now, let's get back to your boundaries, shall we? If our body can tell us when we are full and should stop gorging ourselves, it makes perfect sense that we can identify when we are uncomfortable and a boundary needs to be set. Remember, you are learning a new language. If you miss your "sigh" or choose not to act on it, that's not carte blanche for you to beat yourself up. There's no self-flagellation in boundary setting… something I had to remind myself of just this very morning. I had a little oopsie poopsie slipup and allowed someone else to dictate my boundaries for me. I was dragging out the whipping post when Tom reminded me I was writing a book on boundaries and said, "What would you tell your reader to do in this situation."

Well played, sir. Well played.

Back to your "sigh."

Your internal notification system may show up in a few different ways. Here are some possibilities to get you thinking:

- Disgust. When the phone rings or a text pops up and your face contorts as if you've just stepped in dog puke at 3 am on your way to the bathroom, the call or text is probably from someone with whom you've had boundary issues in the past, and you expect another one is about to happen.

- You delay. Someone asks something of you, and you can't comprehend dealing with the request at that moment. Instead, you put off responding—which is actually worse for everyone involved. When you procrastinate on providing a response, do you suddenly stop thinking about it and go back to your regularly scheduled programming? No! You think about it nonstop. You make it so much worse by putting it off, and it basically consumes your thoughts and your life. If you just tell them you can't (or won't) do whatever it is they need, it frees them up to find someone who can. Ask yourself if your delay is because you want to say no, but you're afraid to.

- Your head is screaming "no." Someone has asked you to do something and your brain is screaming, "Don't do it! Don't agree to that! You don't want to do it! Just say no!" but your mouth hasn't gotten on board with communicating it.

- You can't make a decision. In *Boundary Boss*, Cole says,

139

Word to the wise: indecision is a common experience for women with disordered boundaries. If your boundaries are too loose (porous), you may fear hurting another person or being rejected or ridiculed for a decision. Indecision can be an unconscious way of avoiding that situation. If you deny yourself the right to change your mind, can't speak up, or say no, every decision carries the weight of a life sentence. (40)

- Deja vu. That's right, if you feel there's been a blip in the Matrix, you may have experienced a similar situation in the past. This means you also know how it turned out (and it probably wasn't good). Replay that mental movie real quick and make a different decision to change the ending.

- Your heart starts to pound. Remember, your body may pick up on anxiety before your brain registers it. If you're sweating or feel the physical desire to run, it may be time for a boundary.

Just like in poker every person has a "tell." Learn to recognize your tell.

Of course all of these "indicators" beg the question, "Is this my intuition/gut or my fear talking?" Fear has its place, but if we make decisions through a fear filter, we risk making very poor decisions.

I've mentioned this Inner Matrix program a few times throughout this book, (you can find more information about these classes in the Resources section). It suggests doing some breathwork to put yourself into a "love-based" state before making decisions. It's fairly simple (but boy does it take practice). Do a few rounds of this before you make any decisions.

1. Close your eyes, touch your tongue to the roof of your mouth, and smile. (I know... it feels super weird to smile when you're in a fear state).
2. Breathe in through your nose for four counts.
3. Hold it for two counts.
4. Breathe out through your nose for four counts.
5. Hold it for two counts.
6. Repeat.

Now, if someone is standing in front of you or is on the phone making demands of your time, it's going to look a tad bit bizarre if you close your eyes and do a few minutes of controlled breathing with a fake smile plastered on your face. We are going to talk about Boundary Buffers in more detail in a bit. What you need to know for now is that you can tell someone you'll get back to them, and by then, you'll have an answer. It's okay—I promise.

Practice Makes Perfect (or at Least Better)

I can't stress this enough—you're not going to be great at boundary setting right out of the gate. No amount of Willy Wonka's Veruca Salt whining will make this happen "noowwwww."

A few pointers for how to say no:

- Say no and then uphold it. If you've told someone where your boundary lies and then allow it to be crossed, you will train them to know you *don't* mean business. This will be uncomfortable. Let's say that your mom has a habit of "popping in." You set a boundary and tell your mom that she cannot stop by unannounced and must call before visiting. She agrees, but a few weeks later she's "in the neighborhood" and stops by without so much as a phone call. Upholding your boundaries will mean turning her away and asking her to come back at a time that's more convenient for you.

The person with whom you uphold a boundary may be disappointed, (or you just make up a story about them being disappointed.) Either way, you will have to deal with those feelings.

- Don't assume they know what your boundary is. What we may see as common sense, may not be for someone else. It's our responsibility to communicate our boundaries and to uphold them. Never assume the other person knows what you expect.

   For example, I used to date a man who thought that it was acceptable to have other women sit on his lap when he was out at a bar. I didn't think it needed to be stated that that was not cool. However, it was only common sense to *me*.

   One of my biggest pet peeves is being interrupted when I'm talking. It drives me absolutely nuts. In my past life, I used to work at a mental health facility for the severely mentally ill. I had one client at this job who insisted on busting into existing conversations and starting his own. For some reason I got it into my head that if I ignored someone who was interrupting me, they would figure it out and stop doing it. Behavioral training would support this (if someone doesn't get their desired response, they will change their behavior); but, perhaps, I was asking too much of a client with a severe mental illness.

On this one particular day, I was speaking with another client when he came over and launched into his own agenda. I tried my "behavioral training" method, and maybe it would've worked if I'd had a bit more patience that day. But I was all out of that.

I finally snapped, "You need to wait until I'm done talking to X!"

"Okay. Why didn't you just say that?" he said.

Oops. And that was the day I learned good communication skills from someone suffering from schizophrenia.

We'll discuss specific communication tips in a future chapter.

- Tell them again. Humans have goldfish memories, especially when something is not to their liking. If your boundaries are inconveniencing someone else's pursuit of their agenda, it may be "easy" for them to forget how to treat you. You need to stick to your guns and remind them.

- Practice ahead of time. Get yourself a boundary buddy (more on this in a bit) and practice difficult conversations. It would be great if you could just state a boundary and have it respected and upheld on the first try—but it doesn't always happen like that. Practice conversations and have your buddy push back a bit so you can prepare for how you'll handle it. You may have to say no twice… be ready.

We've spent our lives tuning in to pick up on other people's subtle signals. Now, it's time to tune in to your own. While sometimes you won't understand a boundary is necessary until it's been crossed, the more we learn to listen to our bodies, the easier this whole boundary-setting thing is going to be.

A Note About Dogs

Didn't expect to see this here, did you?

The reason we need to talk about our furry friends for a moment is for many of us we've actually relied on their "gut instinct" more than our own. Allow me to explain.

Back in 2006, my ex and I adopted the sweetest dog ever to have pooped on this earth. Her name was Akasha and she was a Beagle/Lab mix. She loved everyone. She was like the mayor when we'd go for walks. She'd stop to sniff, get pets, and soak up all the attention she could get. She was loved by everyone who knew her, and I don't think she had a mean bone in her body.

Well, we were living in an "apartment community" in North Carolina. I worked out of the house, so I was home all day, and my husband at the time went off to work each morning. The community had a handyman of sorts who would come around once a month changing out the air filters. He was an older gentleman, friendly enough, I guess. But the first time I let him into our home, Akasha positioned herself between us, hackles raised, teeth bared, and tail sticking straight out. When he moved, she repositioned herself directly between us, a low growl escaping from her lips.

I had no idea what she was picking up on, but I was damn sure going to listen. Once the handyman was safely out of the apartment, I let him know that he'd have to call in the future and schedule to come over when my husband was home.

Well, it turns out that what she was picking up on… was probably me. In *The Gift of Fear*, de Becker talks about Ginger, a dog who had a really bad reaction to a woman's new building contractor. "The irony is, that it's far more likely Ginger is reacting to your signals than that you are reacting to hers.

Ginger is an expert at reading you, and you are the expert at reading other people." (33)

So, continue to trust your dog's instincts. Just give yourself some credit, as your dog is just picking up on the instincts you are doing your best to ignore.

Interview with Alex Bratty, MBA, PhD, Founder & CEO of AB Research Consulting

Where do you think your boundaries originated?
I had no idea what a boundary was until I reached my 40s. There was domestic abuse (physical, verbal, and mental) in my home. I never thought about it, but I guess that was a major boundary violation.

A few years ago, I was working as a partner in a research firm and I was putting in 70-80 hour weeks. I worked through vacations; in fact, it became a joke that I was just moving my laptop to a new state. I had no personal life and was on the road most of the time. I was burning out fast. There was a clause in my contract, an escape hatch, that said I could leave (during certain periods) without my non-compete kicking in. I was approaching one of these periods, and I reached out to a life coach to help me decide if I was going to leave and explore what life would look like if I did.

She was the one who introduced me to the concept of boundaries. I responded to clients at all hours of the night and on weekends. The more they expected from me, the more resentful I became. She helped me see (and believe me, it was a bitter pill to swallow) that I had trained my clients to believe I was always available. I had created the nightmare for myself. Once she explained boundaries, I knew she was right.

Are there any beliefs you had to bust through to get where you are now?

My perception of my own worth was tied up in productivity... so I always said yes. My dad called me "stupid," and he was always saying people were "lazy," so I set out to be anything but. I believed that if I wasn't constantly producing, something terrible would happen. I had to prove I could do it all, be successful, be worthy, just to earn the right to be in the world. It sounds crazy when I say it out loud. But I decided early on that I wasn't just going to say yes to everything, I was always going to be the fucking best and blow the doors off.

How do you weigh "opportunities" when they're presented?

I think the very first step is to realize that most "opportunities" are not opportunities. When you approach it like that, it means "yes" is the exception, and the default answer is "no." When someone approaches me, I always pause. I have to put space between the question and my answer.

Next, I evaluate it based off of:
- Is this something I want to do?
- Do I have the time?
- Is it a priority for me?

If the answer to all of those questions is yes, it's a no-brainer, and I'll often agree to it. But if the answer to any one of those questions is no, I have to dig deeper to find out why I'm even considering it.

I've got a backstop question, too: Am I valuing myself and my time if I do this? It's a powerful final check that can often reveal if I'm fooling myself on the first three questions.

What do women need to know as they begin their boundary journey?
First, you have to determine your boundaries. For example, the first boundary I experimented with was telling my clients that I was not available between 7 pm and 7 am.

Second, good communication is a must. People know "how it's always been." If you decide to create a new boundary and change things up on a random Tuesday, you need to let them know the new system—otherwise, how can they know the new boundary exists?

Third, even though it might feel really uncomfortable at first, you have to stick to your boundaries. You can put all this effort into creating one, but if you don't stick to it, the people in your life know that you don't respect yourself, so they don't have to either. One day, I slipped up and read an email at 8 pm. But I kept myself from emailing the client back. If I had, my boundary would've been destroyed.

Fourth, learn to say "no." It's not being selfish. You can even say yes to the person but no to the request. "I love you, and I want to support you, but right now, I have to be here for my own family," is a perfectly reasonable answer.

Finally, when you do well, celebrate it, even if you didn't completely meet your goal (OMG I didn't look at my email for five hours last night). Be compassionate towards yourself and treat yourself for good behavior. Remember, you're training yourself and others on this new way of being.

Back to You

1. How do you physically react when you get a call from a boundary pusher? Take note of the physical sensations in your body, whether you put off responding, have a hard time making a decision, or get that "Haven't I been here before?" feeling.

2. Once you've figured out your "sigh," it's time to pay close attention to when it happens. When you feel yourself reacting, let the person know that you'll need some time before you can give them an answer. Or, if it's a physical boundary that's being pushed, excuse yourself and go to the bathroom to breathe and recalibrate.

Chapter 11:

When the Answer Is Yes (And)

As I mentioned in the Introduction, this book is not designed to turn you into a selfish, self-centered bastard who is unwilling to lift a finger for another human being. I still believe that the greatest joy in life comes from serving others, (especially those of the furry variety). With that being said, there are going to be plenty of times in your life when you say yes—and you mean it!

As a reminder, you'll want to weigh your decision against the Clash Question diagram in Chapter 9. You'll ask yourself:

1. Do I want to/have to do it?
2. Do I have the available resources to do it?
3. Am I willing to give up other things in order to do it?

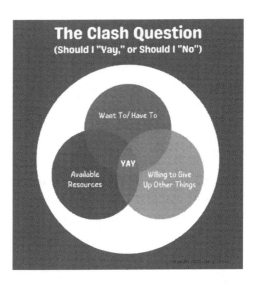

The Clash Question
(Should I "Yay," or Should I "No")

Want To/ Have To

YAY

Available
Resources

Willing to Give
Up Other Things

Allow me to give you an example. In the midst of COVID, a local group was formed to bake cookies for frontline workers. They'd bake and deliver these goodies to nurses, police, nonprofits, and a variety of other people who were making a big difference in our lives during this difficult time. I love to bake and I was looking for a way to help out the community, so I jumped on this opportunity. When I posted it on Facebook, a friend of mine realized how much I enjoyed baking and reached out to see if I could help her, too.

It was Christmas time and she'd agreed to bake seven dozen cookies for an organization she was part of. With a newborn baby at home and her own business to run, she was overwhelmed, over her head, and quickly getting over the holidays. She called me one day in tears. Did I have any time/ desire to bake up a storm?

While I hadn't yet drawn out my diagram, I instinctively used it to make the decision.

1. Did I want to or have to? Absolutely! I love to bake and any excuse to make cookies, (and not make myself and my immediate family fat) was an awesome opportunity.
2. Did I have available resources? Time—check! Money—she was going to pay me for all the supplies, so—check! Emotional—baking cookies is actually soothing to me, so—check!
3. Was I willing to give other things up? Sure. Maybe I missed out on some Netflix time, but I was okay with that.

I said yes. I baked the cookies. I had a blast. Whoever they went to got a delicious dessert. My friend's head didn't explode. And two years later, she still brings that up every time she introduces me to someone.

Saying yes can feel amazing—just make sure it's what you really want to say.

Yes... and

If you've ever taken an Improv class or watched an Improv show, you're probably familiar with the concept of Yes… and. This is one of the pillars of improvisation and is considered an acceptance principle. One of the players creates the reality; for example, they are on a boat. The second player accepts that reality—yes, we are on a boat *and* adds to it, "And it's raining."

This principle helps move the scene along and stops it from becoming an argument between the players in the scene. It also turns out to be a great way to handle boundary setting.

When you agree to do something, it's perfectly acceptable (and a great idea) to add stipulations or conditions to your yes. Remember this is your life, your schedule, and your agenda. Stipulations allow you to help others without inconveniencing yourself.

Let's look at a few types of conditions you may consider adding to your yes:

- Time. Perhaps it's the time you take to attend an event or the order in which you do things. For example; "Yes, I'd love to attend your baby shower on Sunday. And I've got to prepare for the week ahead so I'll need to leave by 5 pm." Or "Absolutely boss, I'd be more than happy to get that project done. And, I'm still working on the other assignment you gave me, so I'll need to finish that first."

- Money. Maybe it's how much you spend on an event or a gift, or perhaps it's lending money to someone you care about. I'm not sure there's a faster way to ruin a relationship than lending money; yet, we are all asked to do it (or ask someone else) at some point in our lives. For example: "I would love to exchange holiday gifts this year. And, I'm on a budget so we'll need to cap the amount at $50 per person." or "Yes, you can borrow money for that class you want to take. And, you'll need to pay me X amount of dollars every month until it's paid back."

- Emotions. If you're like most people, you want to be there for your loved ones. However, there is only so much we can handle at any time. Protecting your emotions could look like this: "Yes, I want to hear all about your Baby Daddy drama. And, I've got a big presentation at work tomorrow that I need to prepare for. Let's have coffee on Saturday, and you can fill me in." You can also put a limit on how much you allow someone to share. I loved this distinction of the different types of complaining in *Set Boundaries, Find Peace*:

> Complaining falls into one of three categories; venting, problem-solving, or ruminating. Venting is a way to

talk about issues without seeking guidance but to simply let out our frustrations. Problem-solving is seeking guidance or advice on how to correct an issue. Ruminating is talking about the same issues over and over without trying to problem-solve or work through your frustrations in any real way. Ruminating is essentially dumping on others. Rarely do I see people have an issue with venting or problem-solving. It's rumination that becomes an issue.

Almost everyone complains about something, but the frequency matters. No one enjoys hearing someone ruminate about the same thing repeatedly. The friend who complains all the time does so without limitation because we have provided space for it. (208)

Complaining is okay to a certain point. But sometimes, it becomes very one-sided. We've all got that friend who launches into a story the moment we answer the phone, "forgetting" to ask if we have time to talk, and "neglecting" to provide a sounding board if we have something to share. It's okay to want your time to vent, too. This could look like:

Friend: "Hey! So I have to tell you about this thing that happened at work today. You're not going to believe it."

You: "Hey there. I'd love to hear about it, and I've actually got something going on in my life right now that I'd really like to share with you. Is it cool if I go first?"

Honestly, your friend may say no. If they do, well, we're going to talk about Boundary Busters in the next section, so stand by.

Another way in which your emotions (and your time) might be tested is "fixing others." Maybe, every time you get on the phone with a friend or relative, they want to discuss someone else. "I just don't know how she's going to make her bills with that deadbeat husband of hers."

In the past, you may have jumped into a 45-minute conversation about how you two could get her a new job or conspire to break up her relationship or just dodge your friend's phone call. Now you know that if someone doesn't ask for help (and sometimes even if they do), it's not your responsibility to fix them. Your conversation may look like this:

"Yes, she is certainly in a pickle. And I want to hear about your life. Tell me how those adorable dogs you rescued are doing."

It's not that you don't want to talk to her or maintain a relationship, it just needs to be on your terms.

When someone hears the word "no," they may become instantly defensive. When they hear the word "yes," it floods their brain with feel-good emotions and positions them to think creatively. However, you don't have to throw your boundaries to the wind when you say yes. Add conditions so that while you're helping someone else, you are still working towards your own goals and not losing sight of your own needs.

Let's take a look at this in the real world.

Not many people know this, but I'm a licensed Wedding Officiant. It started out when I married two chihuahuas for a rescue fundraiser, moved on to a golden retriever and a pit bull as part of a bucket list, and finally, after being asked by several humans, I did what I needed to do to get licensed. Granted, human weddings aren't nearly as much fun as joining pups in furry muttrimony, but my license has come in handy quite a few times.

About two years ago, a friend reached out to me. He was asked to officiate his best friend's wedding, and even though he was a Reverend, he wasn't licensed to perform weddings in Las Vegas. "I'll perform the ceremony," he said. "But would you mind signing the paperwork?"

My stomach instantly clenched. This request made me VERY uncomfortable... but I didn't want to disappoint a friend. Especially one who had put me through his coaching program free of charge, helped me work through some difficult decisions in my life, and had always been there when I needed an ear.

I told him I'd need to think about it and then sat down to do some soul-searching. Why was this bothering me so much? What was the big deal about signing the paperwork when I knew he'd performed the ceremony?

Well, morals. It took me a few days to realize that I'm a bit of a rule follower. When I took my five-hour officiant class, they made it very clear that we were signing a legal document and there were ramifications if we failed to uphold the legality of the situation. Very. Clear.

It's not that I thought a police officer would be stationed at the wedding, waiting to see if I signed the marriage license... but it still felt wrong to me.

Instead of responding with a "no." I utilized a version of the Improv answer. Here's the text I sent:

> **Hey. Ok, I thought about it and talked to a lawyer friend. I'm not comfy just signing off. I'm kind of a stickler for laws and I don't feel right about it. But... options:**

1. I can perform a two-minute ceremony before or after the actual ceremony, (private if they'd like).
2. I can be with you during the ceremony and pipe in to do the actual pronouncement.
3. There's normally a 30-day required lead time to get certified for one ceremony. But they are awesome in that dept. and maybe you can beg them to fast-track you.

I hope this helps. Just let me know if it's option one or two so I can block off that time.

He chose option number one. He performed the ceremony. They walked down the aisle, walked into a separate room. I performed a 45-second ceremony, signed their marriage license, and they were happily married. I kept my friend and my self-respect. Win, freaking, win.

Back to You

1. Looking back on some of the things you've said yes to in the past, where could you have included conditions?
2. How might that have changed the outcome of the situation?

(This exercise isn't to beat yourself up, it's just easier to brainstorm conditions when you're not in the heat of the moment.)

Chapter 12:

Boundaries for the Entrepreneur

I never imagined I'd be starting a chapter about entrepreneurial boundaries with a quote from a fictional prostitute... but here goes.

"I say who. I say when. I say how much."

As Vivian Ward, Julia Roberts' character in *Pretty Women* has some pretty impressive boundaries. She knows her worth and she's not willing to do anything that compromises it. She sets her prices, only works with clients she wants to work with, and refuses to do things outside her "scope," like kissing.

We could all learn a lot from this!

When I first set out to write this book, my intention was to keep boundaries for personal lives and professional lives separate. The more I researched, the more I wrote, and the more I reflected on my own experiences, the more I realized that the two are intertwined and it was naive to think that disordered boundaries get hung up at the office door like a pair of dripping snow boots. No, the way you do anything is the way you do everything. If you have a hard time speaking up for yourself with family and friends, there's a damn good chance the problem is spilling over to work.

In this chapter, we are going to discuss the boundaries you must set as an entrepreneur (or someone working directly with clients). Don't worry if you work in a corporate environment. We'll be discussing communicating boundaries with your coworkers and your boss in the next chapter. You can still learn from the principles we're about to discuss.

Let's start out with a natural segue from your personal life… home offices. If you are like many entrepreneurs (or work from home since COVID hit), you have a room, a corner, or a table in your home dedicated to work. While running your own business affords you the freedom to make your own schedule, it's difficult to establish and maintain boundaries around when you can and can't be disturbed. Your spouse, parents, children, and pets may not understand why you can't give them your full attention. You're home after all.

A friend of mine is a horror writer. She has three children at home, one of which is special needs. If you're thinking to yourself, "That poor woman doesn't get anything done," you'd be wrong. She's written several full-length novels (one of which was nominated for a literary award) and contributed many short stories to anthologies. How does she do it? Bunny ears. Her children know that when mom is wearing the bunny ears, the only time it's acceptable to disrupt her is if the house is on fire or someone is bleeding… like *a lot*.

This author and entrepreneur set up boundaries with her family and with herself. Because of it, she's been successful in her career and has been able to be there for her family.

If bunny ears aren't your thing, that's cool. If you've got a door to close, let everyone know that when it's closed, there's a sign up, or if there's a sock on the handle, there must be fire or blood in order to come in. Even as I sat down to write this chapter, I let Tom know that I was going into "writing mode." He knows this means that I'm going to: put my phone on Do Not Disturb, meditate, and then turn on my music and write. My door is closed. When I'm done for the morning, it will be open again. And lest you think the Do Not Disturb is a boundary for everyone else, it is… but more importantly, it's for me. It's difficult to resist the siren song of an incoming text message. This function blocks them from notifying me so I don't get squirreled every 45 seconds.

"It's okay, I can multitask."

No. You can't. Sorry to be the bearer of bad news. Multitasking isn't actually a thing. It's asking your brain to switch from one task to another quickly. A research study at the University of California, Irvine titled "The Cost of Interrupted Work: More Speed and Stress," found that it takes an average of 23 minutes to get back on task after an interruption. Worse yet, "multitasking" can actually make it *harder* to think. They estimate it's the equivalent of dropping 10 IQ points. I don't know about you, but I'd like to keep all the IQ points I can.

Now, let's discuss clients and customers. No matter what it is you do, there's an end user who pays for it. Clients can be wonderful. They can be infuriating. However, without them, you won't be in business very long. So how do you provide top-notch service without selling your soul?

Did you shout out "Boundaries, motherclucker!"? If so, you're well on your way to success.

Setting expectations is the name of the game. You need to "train" your clients regarding how you work and what you'll put up with. There are a few areas to examine, and if you think back to the six categories of boundaries we discussed earlier in the book, you'll notice the overlap.

When you start working with a client (or when you start establishing boundaries with existing clients), you'll want to communicate:

- When you are available. Including: What are your "office hours"? When are you willing to take calls, respond to texts, or reply to emails?

In Part 1, I talked about a blog client who was making up his own packages. What I didn't mention were the Friday night and Sunday afternoon text messages on top of that. Look, I realize there are businesses out there that need to be on call, ready for an emergency to strike at any moment. Mine is not one of them. I don't think I've ever heard of a life-or-death writing assignment. My clients don't self-destruct if I fail to respond on weekends or holidays, and after years of being "on call" at the animal rescue, physically and emotionally 24/7, I now enjoy my time off.

Am I wrong for wanting to have time to myself? Absolutely not. Should I let clients know that I won't be responding to them outside of normal business hours? Yup. A quick, "I'll get back to you on Monday when I'm in the office," text cleared that up and I actually got a thank you back:

I love your style. I do. I've come to notice your "work hard/play hard" philosophy in life. I admire it. Most people only talk about doing it, but actually doing it is not so easy! In my line of work of 21 years, I've become stuck in the 24/7 mindset, "always open" type of thinking. Thanks

for helping to remind me things can wait until Monday. I'm serious. Thank you for helping me!

- The best way to communicate. What information would you like sent where? For many people, texts or emails become a "paper trail" with important information. If your communications are sometimes through text, sometimes through phone calls, emails, LinkedIn messages, Instagram DMs, or by carrier pigeon or bat signal, it's difficult to keep track. When you let your clients know how to reach you (and you can even share why this method is best), they'll usually respect it.

- Who you will speak with? If there is more than one person attached to the project, maybe partners or an admin, make it clear who you will communicate with and for what purpose.

When I first began working with clients, I agreed to edit a book for co-authors. They were so pleasant on the phone. They'd been friends for years and finally achieved their goal of writing a book together. I was excited about the project.

Until I made an epic oopsie.

"Sheryl, would it be okay if I spoke to you today? Just the two of us?"

If you've ever been in this situation, you know things were about to go downhill FAST. But I had no experience with this and wanting to be agreeable and likable, I said yes. Practically overnight, I became the middleman for those two. The phone calls were frequent, long, and full of complaining about the other person. They played me against each other, both pretending the other person was "the problem," but I could make it all okay.

My attorney friend laughed when I shared my woes over pad thai one day. "I'm sorry you had to learn this the hard way," she said.

Apparently, lawyers, accountants, and marriage counselors all have an ethical obligation not to speak to one co-client without the knowledge and consent of the other co-client. Pity no one stated that ethical obligation for writers. I could've saved almost a year of pain.

When it came time to write *this* book, I reached out to my friend for some practical ideas regarding communicating with clients and crafting contracts. Before I even tell you her name, I must mention the following information should not be construed as legal advice. If you need a contract written, have a dispute with a client or partner, or have any type of legal issue, please seek out the advice of an attorney.

With that being said, I'd like to introduce Jennifer Braster, Commercial Litigator.

"In my eyes, contracts are written boundaries that both parties agree to, in a legal arena, before doing business with one another. A good contract should spell out *everything* in plain English (or legalese) so miscommunications and disagreements can be avoided completely or settled quickly and easily if they do arise."

I'm a trusting person. Too trusting. I used to believe that when people say they will do something, they would actually do it. I've been shown time and time again that that's not always the case. I've learned a lot about contracts the hard way. Not realizing what needed to go into one (or why they are so important) until the damage had already been done. Jen knows this. She's been on the other end of my "OMG what do I do?" phone call on many occasions.

That's why I asked her to provide you with a basic overview of what should be in a contract. And if you're thinking, "I don't really need one for what I do," you're probably just as trusting as I… and you do.

Here are Jen's suggestions (not to be construed as legal advice) for Contracts 101:

- What is the service? With what will you be providing your client? As a writer, I have to include the number of revisions I will do to the work without charging extra. Otherwise, a client could give me edits to make until the end of time.
- What is the scope* of work? What is, and is not, included in the agreed-upon contract?
- What is the time allowance? Is there a set amount of work to be done or will you be working for a set period of time?
- What is the cost of the work?
- How will you get paid? Will you receive a lump sum at the beginning or at the end of the work? Will you receive installments and, if so, how much will each be, and on what date or point of completion will they be delivered?
- Within how many days of invoicing will you be paid?
- If the work exceeds the scope stated in the contract, how will extra costs be calculated? Communicated?
- What are your expectations of the client? Do you need feedback from them? Will they be reviewing progress throughout? Sending you materials? Doing a piece of the work?

- If your business includes materials, exactly what are they getting? Will you be paid when the order is placed or delivered?
- Who will be your point person? This helps outline who you can and can't take direction from. Also, note if there is more than one person and how communication will occur.
- When are you available? Early on in their careers, many professionals will say they can be reached 24/7. As I mentioned before, unless you work in an emergency industry, (medical—the life or death kind, plumbing, bail bonds, tech support for any of the aforementioned industries, etc.), you don't need to be, nor should you be available 24/7. If you've got a client who expects you to be at their beck and call, they aren't the right client for you.
- How long is the contract or package in effect? Do they have a certain period of time to use it? You don't need a client from 10 years ago, popping up and demanding that you finish their project. You could have a full load of work at that point. You could charge A LOT more for the services at this point in your career, as well. You may have even shut down that business and moved on to something else.
- What happens if they continuously cancel appointments? Everyone has (and deserves) an oopsie. Life happens, and emergencies come up. However, your time

is valuable and when someone continuously cancels, it takes away from your success on their project and wastes time you could be spending bringing in more business. Consider a doctor's office or a hairdresser who charges a $25 fee (or more) if you miss an appointment without adequate notice. I (Sheryl) had one ghostwriting client who would text me fifteen minutes before our calls to say he was too busy with work to meet with me. The first time felt like a gift of free time. The second time was a bit irritating. By the 10th or so time, I realized that he had no respect for my time. Put a "missed appointment" penalty in your contract and make sure they understand that "oopsies" don't happen weekly.

- What about showing up late? Just like cancellations, showing up late on a regular basis is disrespectful and has the potential to throw off your entire schedule. Do you have back-to-back calls? Will you shorten your time with the late client or will you push your other clients off 15-20 minutes? Clearly state at what point an appointment needs to be rescheduled.
- What happens if contract terms are not met? You need to give yourself an out if they don't pay as agreed upon, uphold the expectations you've set forth, or turn into a monster who stomps on cities and eats babies. (Those are my words, not hers.)

Under what circumstances can you stop providing your service and are you responsible for returning any money that's been paid up to that point?

* A note about the scope of work. I had never heard this term until, you guessed it, mine was breached. That, my friends, is called scope creep. Allow me to paint a picture for you... literally. You are a mural artist. You put your heart and soul into turning blank walls into beautiful works of art. You are hired to paint a wall in the courtyard of a professional building. You proposed your design, estimated the time and materials it would take you to complete, and set your price, and it was accepted. You got the deposit and used it to buy supplies.

One day, you're peacefully painting in the warm sunshine when you feel someone standing behind you. It's the owner of the building, and he's waiting for you to notice him.

"This is looking great. When do you think you'll have the other walls completed? We've got an event coming up next month and I'll need everything done by then."

You're a little surprised. When you first spoke, you clearly stated that the scope of your work included only the one wall... not the whole courtyard. If you've got great boundaries already, you probably respond with something to the effect of, "Well, I

176

should have this agreed-upon wall completed by next week. I'd be happy to get you some ideas and a quote for the rest of the work. Depending on what you're looking for, I could potentially have it done in time for your event."

Of course, you're reading this book. There's a pretty good chance your boundaries aren't at unicorn level just yet. Which means that conversation would go a bit differently.

"Umm... I mean. I thought we were just doing this one wall. But yeah, I guess I can get that done for you."

Satisfied, the owner walks away while you are mumbling under your breath and calculating how much money you'll be *losing* on this job thanks to the extra time and supplies you didn't budget for. You may even have to push off the start of another job to get this one finished. This is scope creep, both literal and figurative. You agree to do one thing and it turned into something else along the way without so much as a discussion about money.

It happens all the time and a strong contract will prevent that from happening.

One more quick example from the real world. I used to petsit to bring in some extra cash. A friend and fellow petsitter was out of town and asked me to take care of one of her clients. It was just a once-a-day drop-in on a cat, so it should've been a relatively easy job.

Until the owner called me in a panic a few hours into the first day. "I forgot my clothes! You have to go to my house, put some clothing together, and then go to the UPS store and overnight them to me."

Excuse me? I don't have to do any such thing… is what I should've said. But I didn't. Through grumbly breath, I drove to her house for a second time that day, pulled the items she instructed from her closet, drove to UPS, and then SPENT MY OWN MONEY overnighting the package to her.

Let's gloss over the obvious question of how could you possibly go on vacation and forget all of your clothes? Was it my responsibility to do extra work for her? Nope. Would I have if she asked nicely? Absolutely. Should I have told her that I'd be happy to run that emergency errand for her, but I would charge X amount of dollars (above the petsitting fee) to do so? Absolutely.

I lived. I learned. I never pet-sat for her again.

A few more pointers from Jen:

- Include language that any amendments to the contract need to be in writing.

- Have as many phone calls as you'd like, but follow up conversations with an email to document what's been said so there is no confusion.
- If you charge a flat fee for your services, you should still include a maximum amount of hours you will work. Without this, you could end up working til the end of time.
- If materials are involved, consider a UCC Financing Statement. This secures interest in whatever the materials are. This means that if you sell a $50k product to a customer and they try to sell it before paying you, you'll be entitled to be paid from the money they make.
- Finally, there are a ton of templates out on the internet, but for a layperson, the simpler the better. You don't want to put something together if you don't understand what it means. While no new business owner likes the thought of laying out more money in the beginning, if you are starting a business, hire an attorney to draw up a personalized contract template for you. You can edit it for each customer, but you'll have a strong foundation to begin with.

As with any boundaries, professional boundaries are easier to establish at the beginning of a relationship. However, if you're on this journey right now and looking to improve relations with existing clients, do it! Clearly (and kindly) communicate that you've made some changes in your business and these will be the new rules of the road. Truthfully, you may lose a client or two. However, they are probably the clients causing 80% of your stress.

Back to You

1. Are there client relationships in which you've not yet set boundaries?
2. What do you need to communicate to them in order to continue the relationship?
3. What can you learn for your work with future clients?

Chapter 13:

Boundaries for the Employee

"I'm gonna need you to go ahead and come in tomorrow. So if you could be here around 9, that would be great. Oh and I almost forgot, I'm also going to need you to come in Sunday, too. Okay? We, umm, lost some people this week and we need to sort of play catchup. Thanks."

Oh, *Office Space*. Anyone who has ever worked in an office can sympathize with Peter, the main character, who realizes that ever since he started his job every day has been worse than the last.

Imagine for a moment, that instead of grumbling under his breath and dying a little bit inside when his boss Lumbergh destroyed his weekend, Peter responded with, "Actually, I've already got plans this weekend. If you let me know what tasks take priority, I'll adjust my schedule on Monday and get those taken care of for you."

Well, for one, the movie would be horribly boring. But, what are the chances that Lumbergh would fire Peter? More than likely, he'd be disappointed but not wanting to lose a good employee, he'd deal with the no.

Did your heart just stop for a brief moment? Did the thought of saying no to your boss cause you to fan yourself and say in your thickest southern drawl, "Why I never!"? You wouldn't be alone. We (practically all humans, but especially those of us with disordered boundaries) have been conditioned to believe that saying no is not an option at work.

In the last chapter, we discussed how to create boundaries when you own your own business and are your own boss. But what do you do when someone else signs your paychecks? When your manager says jump, are you *really* required to say "how high?" Surely if you say no to your boss, you'll be fired, blacklisted, excommunicated, tarred and feathered, and then burned at the stake.

I don't know your boss, and while you may think that they are *literally the worst,* there's a really good chance that your manager is a human being doing his or her best to get their job done and look good in front of their boss. Are there outliers? Sure. Are there bosses out there who were bullied as children and have risen to a position of power only to abuse their subordinates out of a sadistic need to destroy others? Oh yeah (and I've had one or two of these). Thankfully though, they are not as prevalent as one might think.

These managers create a culture of fear, overwhelm, and dissatisfaction—something I'm going to address in a future book. For now, try out some of the advice that's heading your way, and if it truly doesn't work, it may be time to evaluate your current working environment and start looking for new opportunities.

Okay, with that being said, what do you do when you've been asked to do something by your boss? Looking at the Clash Question diagram, if you've got the time, the bandwidth, and it won't take away from anything else on your plate, it's a no-brainer. But what if your plate is overflowing with responsibilities and adding even the smallest assignment might be the straw that breaks the proverbial camel's back?

To dive deeper, I spoke with Kathi Kulesza, a Leadership Expert with 30-plus years of management experience in the hospitality industry. She cautions that the last thing you want to do is to say yes to something that you won't be able to deliver on. "Not delivering" could look like missing a deadline (which could hold up other cogs in the process); doing a poor job and creating a finished product that is subpar (which reflects poorly on you and the organization as a whole and may cost the business customers or cost you a promotion or even your job); or letting your other responsibilities fall through the cracks (which can cause all of the above problems and more).

Most bosses don't want their employees to feel as if they're being taken advantage of, or not being respected. In fact, most bosses are in the same state of overwhelm as everyone on the team and they are just trying to distribute the work fairly. They expect you to communicate directly, to ask for help if you need it, and to let them know if you can't do something. Sure, you don't want to disappoint people, but by saying yes when you shouldn't, you'll disappoint everyone, including yourself. Show your boss respect and rather than overpromising and under-delivering, allow them to be a part of the decision.

Instead of responding with a blanket yes or (Heavens to Betsy) saying no, Kathi recommends asking questions to determine what's being asked of you and then entering into a negotiation to come to an agreement that works for all parties. Here's a process you can use to uncover the need and find the best solution:

1. Listen when your manager asks you to do something.
2. Repeat back what you've heard to make sure you understand what the project entails.
3. Weigh this request against your workload and consider whether this would prevent you from handling your other responsibilities

or would require you to work overtime. Assuming it would...

4. Ask more about the specifics. Is the due date flexible? Is there someone else on the team that could help with a portion of the work or who would be better suited to take this on? How much overtime is approved (and how much are you willing to work)?

5. Based on this information, could you work on this project once you've finished a current responsibility? Can you team up with another employee and divvy up the work?

6. Let your boss know what projects you are currently working on and ask if you were to take this on would they like to make the decision regarding what should be pushed off in order to get this new project completed or if you should make the decision on your own.

7. Ask if one of your existing responsibilities can be delegated to someone else to make room for the new assignment.

Remember to look at it from your boss's perspective. If they promise their boss that something will be done by a specific time and it's not that will reflect poorly on them and on you. If you accept work you can't get done, everyone looks bad. If you accept work you can't do and force yourself to get it done anyway, you'll be resentful, burn out, and be out the door.

Of course, some of us feel the need to fix everyone else's problems, don't we? When your coworkers are falling behind on a project, they know who to come to. They know that you'll put aside your own work to help them with theirs... and they use this to their full advantage.

Kathi worked with a client just like this. The client would start off the day with the best of intentions but within minutes of reaching her desk, her inbox was full of her coworker's fires. Wanting to please everyone, she'd allow everyone to dump their responsibilities on her, and she'd abandon her plan for the day. She'd then have to work late to get her work done, and instead of enjoying her free time in the evening, she'd be too exhausted to do anything besides open a bottle of wine and melt into the couch. She was overwhelmed, resentful as hell, and considering leaving her job in search of greener pastures.

In their first session, Kathi suggested that she *could* leave, but chances are her "problems" would follow her wherever she went. The issue wasn't that her coworkers were dumping their duties on her. The problem was that she was allowing it. Kathi suggested that for one week she get up early so she could spend some time on self-care and on setting the plan for the day. Then she was to stick to her plan. If she had time left over (and wanted to), she could help her coworkers with their responsibilities—but she had to do hers first. Her client was hesitant but accepted the challenge. At the end of the week, she had more energy, had gotten all of her work completed, AND had the energy to help other people. She stuck with it for a month, and then three… and she no longer wanted to jump ship. There's nothing wrong with showing up for your coworkers. Just make sure you show up for yourself first.

There's nothing I like less than being micromanaged (except maybe Monopoly). When I finished graduate school, I worked for a call center helping loan officers use the company's origination software. Yes, it was as awful as it sounds. But one day… it got worse! I actually really liked my boss. She was fair, didn't hesitate to jump on a call and defend one of her team members, and she loved me because I took the most calls out of anyone in our unit (by A LOT), had the highest ticket close rate, and had the best reviews.

One day, they hired a middle manager who would oversee my department and report to my boss. Looking back, I know she was just trying to make a name for herself and prove that her job was necessary, which it wasn't, but in the moment, I couldn't stand her. She'd hover around my desk and insist that I put my calls on hold to discuss the resolution before I presented it to the client. At the risk of being crass, she was up my butt for three weeks. I was frustrated, my numbers were actually getting worse, and I went home every day in tears.

Finally, I decided that I needed to stand up for myself. I (very respectfully) asked her to leave me alone for one week and then review my performance. If she was unhappy with how I was doing my job, I'd never say another word about her helicopter management. If I was doing a good job, she'd know that she could move on to stalk—I mean, shadow—another employee. She agreed, and a week later she was so pleased with my work, she promised to leave me alone and we actually became friends.

Despite what we've been taught, it's generally acceptable to question authority. The world needs more people who think for themselves, ask questions, and have initiative. Think back to *Office Space* for a moment. When Peter started being honest with "The Bobs" (business consultants brought in to help the company downsize) they didn't fire him… they gave him a promotion and a raise.

Boundaries are not only acceptable at work, they are necessary. In the next chapter, we'll look at some of the ways in which you can communicate your boundaries in the office, in your own business, and in your personal life.

Back to You

1. Make a list of some of the times you have blindly agreed to do something for your boss or a coworker.
2. Take a look at each individual situation and brainstorm how you could have used one of the techniques above to prevent yourself from becoming overworked and probably underappreciated.
3. Find a friend to work with. Have them role-play your boss and ask you to do something. Practice asking questions and making suggestions that would work better for you and for your boss.

Chapter 14:

Communicating Your Boundaries

At the end of *The Muppet Christmas Carol* (and probably the actual *A Christmas Carol*—but I've never seen that), Scrooge has been through his ghost-induced transformation and stops by the Cratchits on Christmas Day.

Emily Cratchit (Miss Piggy) has had enough of this miserly bastard mistreating her husband. When Bob Cratchit (Kermit) answers the door and proves that he is once again NOT going to stand up to his boss, she stands by her frog and lets Scrooge have it.

While her show of Boundary Buddy support is strong (more on that in the next chapter), her communication skills are a bit lacking and she almost misses the part where Scrooge offers to give Bob a raise and pay off their mortgage.

When you wake up from decades of living a boundaryless life, it's easy to approach communicating your new parameters like a bull in a china shop. Easy, but not useful. In this chapter we're going to discuss some communication do's (and don'ts) for having new conversations. We're also going to break down the boundary-adjacent situations in which you may have to participate.

Preparing for the Conversation

If you are a musician, you practice for a gig. If you are an actress, you practice before getting on stage. If you are an athlete, you practice before the big game. If you are a chef, you practice before the restaurant opens. Are you noticing a pattern?

There's no need to go into a boundary conversation cold. Grab yourself a friend, colleague, or family member who can run through it with you. Ask them first to accept what you've got to say and then offer some pushback so you get experience dealing with that as well. Practice a few times. Then, practice on your own. Say it in front of a mirror until the words roll off your tongue instead of getting stuck in the back of your throat. Will you look silly repeating "No" into a mirror? Possibly. Will you feel better when it comes to the main event? Absolutely.

Once you've got your practice rounds in, it's time to approach your conversation partner. How and when you do this will directly impact the outcome of your chat. Set the stage properly and you are likely to be well-received. Approach this Miss Piggy–style and you'll probably have a damaged relationship on your hands.

First, make sure you are in private. (Unless you are dealing with a dangerous individual. If that's the case, please speak to a professional therapist before utilizing any of the following advice.) Do you remember wanting to crawl into a hole when the teacher called you out in front of the entire class? Or how you hoped lightning would strike you dead when your boss commented negatively on your performance in front of your team or customers? Don't do that to others. Ask to speak to them privately before you air your grievances.

Next, ask permission. I know, it sounds silly that you should have to ask someone if it's a good time to talk. However, if you've ever walked into a room where your partner is watching their favorite show and tried to have a conversation, you know that the other person needs to be *ready* to talk. The flip side of that is they may not be in a good space to have the conversation. A really bad day at work, not feeling well physically, getting bad news about a relative—there are a number of things that would render someone temporarily incapable of this kind of conversation.

Choose your time wisely and make sure the other person is available to receive what you have to give.

Do's

Now that you've properly set the stage for the conversation, let's take a look at what you can do to help things go smoothly.

- Breathe. Take a few deep breaths before you begin. If you feel yourself getting emotional during the talk, take a breath and center yourself. The calmer you are, the better this will go.
- Pause. This ties into breathing. Pause throughout the talk to give the person time to digest what you are saying and, once you've said your peace, pause to give them an opportunity to respond.
- Be mindful of your body language and tone. The words you've chosen to use may convey confidence, but if your shoulders are slumped, you're looking down, or your voice is low and wobbly, confidence will not be what they hear.
- Be clear and directly state your request. It may be tempting to soften the blow with lots of extra words and fillers like, "Do you know what I mean?," but the only thing these will serve to do is confuse the other person and weaken your message.
- Deal with the discomfort. This is huge. The first couple (or hundred) times you set a boundary, you are going to feel icky. You may experience guilt at saying no. You may

feel sad that you can't be there for someone in the way you've always been. You may have a wave of, "Who the hell am I to stand up to them." The feelings will be plentiful and many will not be pleasant. That's okay. A few moments of discomfort are going to make a world of difference in your future. Feel the discomfort. Accept it. And then let it know that while you appreciate it notifying you that the status quo has been breached, it can take a hike.

Don'ts

With your best practices locked and loaded, let's look at what to avoid during these conversations.

- Don't assume they'll react a certain way. I know you've been playing this conversation out in your head, and you're expecting the worst. They'll probably disown you. They'll for sure tell you to "f" off. They might even sprout horns, have flames shoot up behind them, and growl at you in a devil's voice. Are you done? Can we put an end to the Disasterpiece Theatre going through your head? I've been there (and may I say I can be quite creative when it comes to the worst-case scenario). However, what you *think* will happen and what is likely to *actually happen* are usually worlds apart.

Don't go into this conversation bracing for impact.

- Don't assume they know what you mean. As we discussed in the Do's, you need to be clear and concise. When you get all flowery to cushion the blow, you'll probably lose them. Be clear and then ask them to tell you what they heard. That's when you'll find out how you did and how your message was received.
- Avoid absolutes. Ever been in a conversation (on either side) that involves statements like "You never" or "You always?" Whether the never or always is in fact true or not (and it's usually not), it sounds like a four-year-old throwing a tantrum. In the next section, we'll discuss how to provide specific details to back up your emotions.
- Don't vomit an explanation or an excuse. While it's okay to give a reason for why you're saying no (I have too much on my plate at work, my daughter is sick and I need to be there for her, or I already have plans and it wouldn't be fair for me to cancel them), it's not required. You actually don't *owe* anyone an explanation. And you certainly don't owe them a long one.
- Don't interrupt. If you want people to hear you out, show them the same courtesy. Plus, much like the Miss Piggy vs. Scrooge example, they might be trying to say

something you actually want to hear like, "I'm sorry, I didn't realize that bothered you. I won't do that in the future."

- Don't apologize. I left this one for last even though it might be the most important "Don't." You have every right to say no. You have every right to let people know when something they've done has negatively affected you. You have every right to speak your mind and have your voice heard. And you don't need to apologize for it.

In *The Assertiveness Guide for Women*, de Azevedo Hanks says,

> Having strong boundaries requires you to mean what you say and stand your ground. Sometimes women have a tendency to apologize for things that don't warrant an apology. Have you ever said anything potentially assertive and/or uncomfortable by starting with, "Hey, sorry to bother you, but…" or "Sorry, hope this isn't weird…"? I think one of the main reasons we unnecessarily apologize is because we are afraid of coming off as intimidating or intrusive. But keep in mind that your voice deserves to be heard and valued just as much as the next person's. Incessant apologizing may undermine your message or weaken your boundary. Save your sorries for when you've truly done something

wrong, not for when you make valid assertions by sharing your feelings, thoughts, wants, and needs, or expressing difference. (168)

With that being said, there is a time when you should apologize... when you've crossed someone else's boundary. I've got a friend who gets creeped out by two specific words. They upset him and he's pointed it out to us all multiple times. But it's funny to see him get creeped out. They aren't universally offensive words, he just doesn't like the sound of them.

For years, we've all teased him with these words and delighted as we watched him turn into a puddle of discomfort. Well, as I was researching and outlining this book, I realized that I was crossing a mental/emotional boundary. We were out to dinner with him last week, and I accidentally said one of the words. It was truly an accident and came up in conversation, but it reminded me that I had some apologizing to do.

"I'm truly sorry for all the times I've made you uncomfortable, knowing how you feel about it. You have my word that going forward, I will never do that again."

Apology accepted (although it shocked the crap out of him). When you are the one who has crossed a line, make it right.

Okay, let's get back to communicating your boundaries, shall we?

Situational Conversations

There are a few different boundary-related conversations you may need to have going forward. We are going to break those down so you are prepared for (almost) anything that comes your way.

1. Setting Expectations at the Beginning of a Relationship
2. Communicating That a Boundary Has Been Crossed
3. Setting Boundaries or Communicating Needs During a Relationship
4. Saying No

Setting Expectations at the Beginning of a Relationship

Obviously, this is the best time to have a conversation around expectations. When a relationship is new (it doesn't matter whether it's personal or professional), you have not yet trained the person regarding how to treat you. It's like a fresh slate for both of you.

When it comes to work, let your coworkers or clients know when you are available. Put it in your contract, include it in your onboarding conversation, and just let them know in no uncertain terms when you are available to help them and when (barring an emergency) you are tending to the other areas of your life.

Communicating boundaries early on in your personal life is essential, as well. You can be there for friends, but is it acceptable to call you at midnight to talk about daily drama? Probably not. In this case, you could let friends know you "unplug" at 8 pm so you can unwind from the day.

The earlier you have these conversations, the less "untraining" you'll need to do.

Communicating That a Boundary Has Been Crossed

While living your boundaryless existence, you may have known when something was awry... or you may not have. Now that you are educating yourself on the way of the boundary samurai, it's pretty clear when someone has overstepped. While it may seem like a bad thing (you mean I actually have to *feel* and *stand up for myself*???), it's actually a wonderful step in your evolution.

When someone does something that crosses your newly formed or identified boundaries, you need to tell them. Once again, Miss Piggy's zest will not serve you well. You may be tempted to start screaming, "You made me so angry, you obnoxious, demanding buffoon!," but don't. That will just put the other person on the defensive and really does anyone use the word "buffoon" these days?

Instead of attacking, lead up to the conversation with an ice breaker like:

- "I thought you should know."
- "I need to make you aware of my feelings about what happened."
- "I wanted to bring something to your attention."

And then try this helpful formula:

I feel _____ when you _____ because I think _____.

First, some examples. Then, we're going to break down why this is awesome.

- I feel angry when you correct me in front of our friends because I think you believe I am not intelligent.

- I feel sad when you don't call when you promised to because I think you aren't concerned about my well-being.
- I feel frustrated when you call my personal cell on weekends regarding work matters because I think you don't respect my need for downtime.

Okay, why does this work?

- "I feel" is a lot different than "I am." The former puts distance between you and the emotion making it an experience, not an identity. The latter turns you into the Hulk and requires that you yell, "Hulk Angry," and rip your shirt off. Okay, it doesn't *require it,* but it does suggest it.
- "I feel" is different from "You made me" because you are not putting the responsibility of your emotions on someone else. No one is responsible for your emotions but you. Don't give them that power, mmkay?
- "When you…" points to a specific behavior or moment in time. It avoids the Don't we mentioned earlier regarding "always" and "never."
- "Because I think…" gives the other person insight into what you're hearing and how you are interpreting their words and behavior.

- The entire formula conveys that you are a mature adult capable of clear thought and communication, rather than a child who is controlled by their emotions and left with no tools other than to shout, "You... you... you stupid head!"

Setting Boundaries or Communicating Needs During a Relationship

Perhaps you've heard the Chinese proverb, "The best time to plant a tree was 20 years ago. The second best time is now."

Well, obviously the best time to set a boundary is before it becomes an issue. But, the second best time is now. It's never too late to ask for the treatment you deserve. It is important, however, to remember that you have trained the other person as to what's acceptable behavior so you can't hold them fully responsible (yet) for their behavior.

Once you've utilized the formula above to let them know a line has been crossed, you'll need to clearly identify what you expect in the future. You can use starters such as:

- "In the future..."
- "Going forward..."
- "When this situation comes up again..."

- "I would appreciate it if you don't..."

Then, let them know *exactly* what you want them to do differently. Maybe you'd prefer they correct you in private (or not at all). Maybe you'd like them to call or text to check on you twice a day while you are sick and living alone. Or perhaps you'd like them to refrain from contacting you on your cell outside of regular business hours (and state what those are for your industry).

You have the opportunity to strengthen your relationship at any time. Embrace that. Now, it's important to note that you can *ask* for any type of treatment you want. That doesn't, however, mean you are going to get it. There will be people in your life who are unwilling to alter the way they behave, and frankly, you have no control over that. What you do have control over is whether you allow them to remain in your life. In Part Three, we're going to talk about what to do with Boundary Busters.

Before we hop over to the grand poobah of boundary setting—the NO, let's talk about how to communicate your needs to people. I have to defer to the most common (and stereotypical) example here.

There's a great video floating around called, "It's Not About the Nail." You see a couple talking while the camera focuses from their eyebrows down. The woman is saying things like, "There's all this

204

pressure, it's relentless. And sometimes, I'm afraid that it will never go away."

At this point, the camera pans over and you see that the woman has a nail sticking out of her forehead.

Her partner responds with, "Well, you do have a nail sticking out of your head. I bet if we got that out, it would all go away."

"It's not about the nail," she says, completely exasperated by the conversation. "Stop trying to fix it!"

He finally gives up and listens to her complain about how all of her sweaters are snagged and says, "I'm so sorry. That must be really difficult for you."

The video is hilarious, but it also perfectly shows what happens when you don't let someone know what you need ahead of time.

Have you got a "fixer" in your life? They may be a partner or friend of the male persuasion or they could be a well-meaning, future-focused woman. You come to them with a problem, and truthfully, you just need to vent. You aren't looking for 201 ways to fix your situation. You just need five solid minutes of bitching and then you can move on with your life.

Of course, that's not their default setting. Let them know. Preface your conversation with what you need. "I'd love to get your feedback on something," vs. "I just need you to listen." Trust me, you'll both be much happier that the expectation is set early on, and there's no frustration or resentment after the fact.

Saying No

We're here! We're here! It's the moment you've been waiting for. We're about to dive into how to say no to something you don't want to do. By now, you've probably ascertained that no is a complete sentence and a completely acceptable answer. However, for many of us, it still feels harsh and doesn't appeal to our delicate sensibilities. All good. I've got you covered. Here are a few ways you can drop a no-bomb with little to no collateral damage.

- I'm not able to commit to that right now.
- I'm honored that you would ask me, but the answer is no.
- That's just not going to work for me.
- I'm not able to support you in that way.
- I want to, but I'm unable to.
- I really appreciate you asking me, but I can't do it.
- I understand you really need my help, but I'm not able to do that for you.

If you'd like to add a quick "why," that's okay (but not necessary). If you'd like to leave the door open with a "...right now, but keep me in mind for the future," you can (but it's also not necessary). And if you'd like to use the Improv technique in the last chapter to say that you will help them and then outline the conditions, you can (but it's still not necessary). Say no. Stick to your guns. People may not like it, but if they care about you and value the relationship you have, they will respect it.

You may at some point find it necessary to say no to answering inappropriate questions or you may have to tell someone to stop giving you advice. This doesn't have to be a hugely dramatic interaction. You can kindly shut them down and then distract them with another topic. For example:

- "I don't want to talk about that. But I would love to hear about your new job."
- "While I appreciate your advice, I'm prepared to figure this out on my own. How was your vacation?"

If you just try to distract them, you won't get your point across and they'll likely keep coming at you. If you shut them down and then distract them, any mention of it after the fact is inappropriate. Hold your stance and repeat what you've said. They'll either get the idea and take your ushering into a new conversation or that conversation will end. It's a win either way.

One last thing before we move on to a new topic. Throughout this chapter, we've been talking about ways to communicate boundaries with the people in your life with whom you'd like to maintain a relationship. Not everyone will fall under this category. There are some people who do not deserve your kindness, your politeness, or your attempts at diplomacy. They may be endangering your safety or well-being. They may be complete strangers trolling on the internet (or in real life). When it comes to dealing with these people, I couldn't possibly put it any better than they did in *Stay Sexy & Don't Get Murdered*:

> Sometimes responding to the world and people and difficult citations with bravery and confidence feels impossible. Fucking politeness isn't a strict rule, it's a practice, an art to master throughout your life. Think of it like a weapon you carry in your pocket. With practice (and I recommend practicing on dudes in bars who really want to buy you shots), you'll learn to wield that weapon like a fucking ninja in order to protect yourself. Throughout your life, you'll master knowing what situations call for what level of fucking politeness. This is why it's so important to recognize red flags for what they are: warning signals that when paid attention to

are basically crystal balls into what level of "ga fuck yaself" is necessary. (Kilgariff & Hardstark, 48)

Well put, ladies. Well put.

Interview with Jennifer Scher – Executive Director at a Jewish nonprofit, wife, and mother of three

Where do you think your boundaries originated?

I don't remember boundaries being something we discussed when I was growing up. I learned them when I started in my first professional role. I've had some really great mentors throughout my career. In 2007, I started working at the Jewish Federation as a fundraiser and engagement coordinator. One of the community Rabbis invited me out to lunch. "I'm going to tell you something, and you can take it or not. The Jewish community will eat you alive. I'm not going to tell you how many nights you are willing to work, but you need to figure out how many and then draw the line."

I spoke with my husband. We decided that two nights a week (with three during gala season) was perfectly reasonable. I clearly stated my boundary to colleagues early on, and they accepted it.

Are there any beliefs you had to bust through to get where you are now?

I wasn't a stellar student. People have always underestimated what I'm capable of, and for a while, I did too. There were very low expectations for women when I was growing up. Certainly, no one expected me to go into an executive role in a nonprofit. When you're ambitious and want to go into a C-suite position, people just don't know how to react to it.

How do you weigh "opportunities" when they're presented?

My organization is often approached for partnership opportunities. When it comes to my schedule, I weigh the opportunities as part of a full week's schedule. Can I handle it that week? Will it benefit the organization? Generally, my default answer is yes; however, I only have that freedom because I have a team. I can agree to something and then delegate it to one of my employees.

When it comes to my personal life, I love to get together with people. However, my friends know that I reserve the right to cancel at the last minute. My oldest son has autism, and things can turn upside down real fast. All I have to say is, "I can't come. Having an autistic day," and people understand.

What do women need to know as they begin their boundary journey?

It's good to set the stage early on. I start out conversations with potential donors by saying, "Part of what you need to know about me is that I'm a mom." I teach them that between the hours of 5:30 pm and 7:30 pm, that's time to be with my family. I'm feeding the kids, getting them ready for bed, and spending quality time. Unless it's an emergency, even the highest donors don't contact me.

Consider what you share and with whom. My husband and I made an agreement early on. We limit what we share with our families. They don't need to know every time there's a meltdown or drama in our personal or professional lives. We stick to that agreement, and the trust we've created has made our relationship stronger. Trust makes all relationships stronger.

When it comes to saying no... just say no. There's no need to feel guilty. I believe in being supportive, collaborative, and helpful to colleagues, but there's a line. I refuse to have my time taken advantage of.

Back to You

The sentence starters I've suggested in this chapter aren't for everyone. Write out a few ways to communicate your boundaries that sound and feel like you. If you're comfortable with the verbiage, you'll be more comfortable speaking to people.

Chapter 15:

Boundary Buddies—The People You Surround Yourself With

A few years ago, my friend dubbed me her official "No Woman." At that point, she was saying yes to *way too many* "opportunities" and was getting overwhelmed with all the volunteer work she'd taken on. Between her church, Toastmasters, and her professional organization, she had no time to advance her business or sleep.

"Just send them to me," I said whenever she was contemplating saying yes again. And one day, she took me up on it.

I received a call from a mutual friend. "Sheryl, I'm not sure why, but our friend told me to call you."

"Hmm… did you ask her to do something?"

"I did! I need someone to cover the meeting on Friday."

"Well, that's why she told you to call me. Yeah, she's not going to do that."

We had a good laugh, and he accepted the "no." I called her with the results. We decided that I'd be known henceforth as Jiminy Cricket, her external consciousness. Or at least her external boundary setter. A lot of people have them.

Rumor has it that as Ellen DeGeneres walks through crowds, she's asked to do a lot of stuff for fans, (i.e., show up for parties, write the foreword to a book, endorse their product, etc.). She graciously accepts every offer. Of course, right behind her is the "No Woman." She does just what I did for my friend: "Yeah, she's not going to do that."

Eventually, when you set your own boundaries enough, you're not going to need a Jiminy in your life. However, no matter how long you've been working with boundary setting, it will always help to surround yourself with helpful people.

I like to call these Boundary Buddies. These are the people who:

- You can talk to when you have a decision to make.
- Provide an outside perspective.
- You can "blame" when taking time to respond and saying no.
- Understand what your response delays really mean and create a safe space for you to say no.

Let's take a look at a few examples:

- I have a lot of respect for my cousin. She's managed to work in the nonprofit field for most of her career while a) making a reasonable salary and b) maintaining a separation between work and home life. When I have a question about boundaries, I'll call and run the situation by her. Her insight is usually helpful and, while I may not come up with a decision on the spot, her input definitely impacts the direction I move in.

- Perhaps you just need a boundary buddy to point out (after the fact) when a boundary has been crossed so you can either a) fix it or b) learn from it moving forward. There are many times when I'll be sharing a story with Tom or a friend of mine and get met with a puppy head tilt and an "umm, that's kind of f'd up." Sometimes, we don't realize boundaries have been crossed until someone else points it out for us.

- I was single for about 14 years (give or take a few relationships) in my adult life. I chose how to spend my money, my time, and my energy, and didn't need to consult anyone before making a decision. While it may sound great to some readers, when it comes to boundaries, it turns out that making decisions as a couple is WAY easier.

Tom is incredibly generous with his money. This is a beautiful thing… until it isn't. Unfortunately, he can be *too* generous and, sometimes, he gets taken advantage of. When he would go on vacation with friends, he'd actually *take* them on vacation—all expenses paid. If someone asked to borrow money, he was standing by with cash in hand.

When we moved in together and began commingling our bills, he was excited to institute a monetary clause: before spending more than our agreed-upon limit, we need to check with the other person. "That way, I'll have to think before spending," he said.

Having lived on a budget most of my life, I'm way more generous with my time. The first time I agreed to dogsit after we'd moved in together, he asked, "Shouldn't you check with me before bringing another dog into the house?" Hmm… I guess I should.

This works out great. No longer can we have knee-jerk reactions to whatever people ask of us. There's a built-in Boundary Buddy we need to "consult" before we can say yes. This leaves plenty of time to assess the situation, run through the

Clash Question, and determine whether we want to say no, yes, or yes with conditions.

Don't have a significant otter (still not a typo) to consult with? That's okay. Your knee-jerk response can now be, "I have to check my calendar" or "I have to look at my budget." Anything that buys you time to breathe, evaluate, and formulate the appropriate response is going to be a win.

Oftentimes, your friends or loved ones are going to be the ones asking you to do things you may not want to do. Surround yourself with people who know your tells. For example, if you have to ask me 15 times if I want to do something, I don't. A good friend will recognize that and stop pushing. Of course, you can't rely on that 100% of the time. That's why learning to set your own boundaries is so damn important.

Finally, I would be remiss not to mention the dark side of who you surround yourself with. Just like misery loves company, dysfunctional boundary-ites (new word—feel free to use it) surround themselves with other dysfunctional boundary-ites. Often, when you fail to enforce your own boundaries, you're not very good at accepting other people's boundaries either. We're going to talk about this more in the next chapter.

Back to You

1. Make a list of the Boundary Buddies you can count on to give you advice, perspective, and a scapegoat.
2. Consider the people you spend the most time with—do they have healthy boundaries or are you all just feeding off of each other and spiraling into a pit of boundaryless despair?

Chapter 16:

Other People's Boundaries (OPB)

"If you want friends, be a friend. If you want good friends, be a good friend."

You've likely heard this (or seen it stitched on a pillow in Hallmark), and hopefully, you've taken it to heart. However, did you ever consider what this means for the wonderful world of boundaries?

If you disrespect people's time; borrow money or personal effects without returning them or return them broken or stained; complain nonstop and don't let them get a word in; or hug them when they don't like to be touched, do you really expect them to respect your boundaries once you set them?

The fact is, sometimes people aren't going to be able or willing to help us in the way we want to be helped. Sometimes, their priorities don't align with ours and they'll choose themselves over us. And… we need to be okay with that.

About two years ago, I was asked to foster a pup named Buddy. His mom was in the hospital and the rescue didn't want to leave him at the shelter over

Christmas. I had just lost Akasha, my Beagle/Lab mix and my best friend of 15 years, so I said if Bodhi, my little old man, didn't mind, Buddy would have a home for the holidays.

I brought this fuzzy-faced terrier mix home, and Bodhi didn't seem to care one way or another. We were past Christmas day when I found out that his mom wasn't just in the hospital, she was also homeless. The two of them had already spent a night at the homeless shelter. I held on to Buddy for a few months while she got back on her feet—and every time she fell off them again. I fell in love with Buddy and he became a part of my family. For two years, I was his "furry godmother" and would take him in when needed, bring him supplies, and get his medical needs taken care of. When Tom and I got together, he fell in love with Buddy too.

Well, in July of this past year, his mom texted to say she was moving them to Colorado. I panicked. I would no longer be able to get to him quickly in an emergency. I got him a tag with my information and I began looking for "boots on the ground" in case he needed me. Thereafter, whenever I learned that someone lived in Colorado, my first question was, "Would you be able to get to a dog quickly in an emergency?"

I eventually realized that I do know a few people in Colorado through the Inner Matrix program. I had already gotten one call that Buddy and his mom were sitting outside a liquor store in Colorado Springs and his mom was bleeding. I knew it wouldn't be long before "the" call came. I immediately shot off a text to one of the women in the program and explained the situation.

"Hey, is there any chance you'd be able to pick up the dog and hold on to him for a day or two until I can get out there?" She said she'd have to check with her partner, as they'd just lost their dog and it may not be a good time. I waited patiently… sort of. More like I combed my Facebook friends to see who else might be willing and able.

She responded the next day, "I'm sorry. I can't support you in that way right now."

In my heart, I thought, "Wait? What? Do you not understand that this is the best dog in the world? Do you not understand that he needs help? All he's been through? What could happen to him if I don't get to him quickly enough?"

But, as Madam Working on Boundaries, I opted to respect her boundaries and respond with, "I understand. Thank you for letting me know."

Sometimes it truly sucks to accept other people's boundaries. But, you've got to be down with OPB. I'm sorry, I couldn't pass up that opportunity.

In case you're wondering, "the" call did come. We found someone to pick up Buddy and keep him safe while Tom and I canceled everything, threw an overnight bag in the car, and drove the 12 hours to Colorado (and then the 12 hours back). Buddy is now sleeping soundly on the couch, a sloth stuffy nuzzled under his front leg.

One more example before we move on.

Las Vegas has grown quite a bit since I've been living here. It used to take around 20 minutes to get anywhere in this valley. My mom raised me to believe that unless you are two hours early you are late. In fact, she once arrived at the airport to pick me up before my flight had even left. I carried this early-bird-itis with me for years. But somewhere between becoming hellaciously busy and packing way more into a day than anyone can actually do, and the traffic getting so bad in Las Vegas that it now takes 40 minutes to get anywhere, I lost that quality.

I didn't set out to be late everywhere but, sure enough, I was.

My friend George was coaching me for a speech contest and we had a 1 p.m. practice session scheduled at his house. Not only was I running about 15 minutes behind, but it turns out that we had agreed on 12 o'clock for the practice session, not 1. Oops.

I arrived 80 minutes late to a very (justifiably) irate George. "Do you realize that you've thrown off my entire schedule and sent the message that my time is not valuable?"

Well, I didn't before… but I certainly did after. I apologized profusely, realized that I had disrespected him and his boundaries, and vowed never to do it again. And I haven't.

If you want others to respect your boundaries, you have to respect theirs.

Interview with Katie Perry, Managing Partner with Jamison Perry Staffing (JP), Director of Member Experience for the International Association of Women (IAW), military wife, and mom.

Where do you think your boundaries originated?

I grew up with a stubborn personality. I think I naturally put boundaries in place because I wanted things to go the way I wanted them. It wasn't until later in life that I realized how to utilize boundaries to support myself and the people around me. Too often, when we talk about boundaries, we only think about the ramifications for ourselves. But there's a ripple effect.

When I say yes to something, I say no to something else. There's no vacancy for that to happen, so who does it affect? If I say yes to something with IAW, I have to say no to something at JP. If I say yes to something at IAW or JP, I may have to miss out on something with my family.

We can take that even further. When we say no to something, say a request to serve on a board or lead a project, we are giving someone else an opportunity. I could've done it, though something else might get compromised. In the end, it could serve someone else better than me.

Are there any beliefs you had to bust through to get where you are now?

I've struggled with all the common themes—"I'm not enough," "Not pretty enough," "Not smart enough," "I didn't come from a wealthy family"—but I like to think that adversity is what made me who I am today. We need to embrace what those beliefs teach us. We need to accept where we come from and figure out how we can build on it.

How do you weigh "opportunities" when they're presented?

I found a great strategy that Brendon Burchard recommends for determining

whether or not you should move forward
with an opportunity.
(https://brendon.com/blog/evaluate-opport
unities)

TERMS < ROI + FV + L + PD
- TERMS stands for: Time, Energy,
  Resources, Money, Sanity.
- ROI is Return on Investment (does
  it save time, build energy or
  resources, or increase money?)
- FV is Future Value (will you benefit
  from it in the future)
- L is Lifestyle (how will this change
  your lifestyle? Added work hours?
  Time away from family?)
- PD is Personal Development (does
  this make me who I want to be?)

I always weigh all the variables and take
stock of my needs and priorities. For
example, I had season tickets to the Silver
Knights (hockey) game the other night. I
had no other commitments, and I'd already
spent the money. But after planning a
huge gala this past week and the
pressures of my business, I needed some
quality time in my sweatpants. Sure, I
could've met someone and created
business at the game. I would've had fun
and I wouldn't have wasted the money I'd
already spent, but the downtime was more
important.

What do women need to know as they begin their boundary journey?

You need to be comfortable having your own boundaries, but you also need to be graceful in accepting them from others. If we were always met with "I support you," we'd have an easier time setting them.

I invited a friend to the gala. She was trying to make it work in her life but ultimately sent me a text the day before that she couldn't attend. She explained how there was just too much going on and finished the text with, "Still love me, k?"

My heart broke a little. Not because she couldn't attend but because she thought it would damage our friendship. I responded with, "Part of being a good friend is supporting friends when the answer needs to be no. If that is what your life needs right now, I support you."

Sometimes, being a good friend means helping someone else establish a boundary. Over the years, I found that people volunteer for roles out of the goodness of their hearts. But when life changes and the responsibilities become overwhelming, they don't see an exit. Be willing to recognize when you have to help someone else. I tell people that if the role is no longer a good fit for them, I can help them transition out... and I'll still love them. You can see and hear the sigh of relief when they realize you're there to support them.

So many of our battles are because we're afraid of how others will receive us. You're not going to be everyone's cup of tea in this life, and that's okay. When you get comfortable enough in your own skin to put action behind the things you say are important, you're going to be a happier human. And you're not always going to get it right. Even with great boundaries, you're going to mess up. That's okay.

Back to You

1. Think about the people in your life. Have you neglected to respect their boundaries?
2. If so, come clean! Do you owe them an apology or is there something you can do to make it up to them?

Part 3:
Boundary Reflections

Chapter 17:

Celebrating Successes

Whether you were "today days old" when you learned about boundaries or you've been aware of them for years (though maybe not so good at setting them), chances are you've set a boundary or two in your life.

There are two aspects to this chapter. The first is celebrating the boundaries that we've set in the past, studying who they were with, and what made them possible and successful (even if only to a certain degree). Through our past, we can learn where we need more work and how we can improve in our everyday boundary setting.

The second aspect of this chapter is to celebrate the boundaries we set moving forward. This isn't just a new language we're learning, it's a new muscle we're training. You wouldn't expect to go to the gym once, hit the weights really hard, and look like Arnold Schwarzenegger in the early '70s (or his female equivalent). At least, you *shouldn't* expect that. Just like training your body, training your boundary muscles is going to take time. There are going to be some days you feel like a weightlifting rockstar. There will be some days when you can't lift shit. And, there will be some days that you're so sore you can barely get out of bed. I'm going to challenge you to learn from the bad days but focus on the good days. And… celebrate!

Let's jump into how to dissect your past successes and learn from them.

While my divorce was fairly smooth (no kids and no money), the reason for it was a few cameras short of *To Catch a Predator*. I won't go into it here. (You'll have to read *Surviving to Thriving: How to Overcome Setbacks and Rock Your Life* for the full scoop.)

But afterward, I dragged my butt to therapy a few times a week, read ALL the self-help books, did the inner work, and came out of the ordeal relatively unscathed. Don't laugh… I said "relatively." While my ex is the butt of many jokes, I rarely think about him outside of that, and the emotions have all been dealt with.

Which is why I was so damn curious when I got a Facebook message from his current wife. I've since deleted it, but the gist was, "Hi, this is X's current wife. I'm about to file for divorce and I was hoping to talk to you before I serve him with the papers."

Ummm…. Whaaaaaat? I was the cat, and curiosity was about to take me down. I responded and agreed to get on the phone with her. You don't need to know all of the details, just know that he had woven quite the tale of fiction and fantasy, and she'd bought into every bit of it.

"I just wanted to hear your side of the story," she said about halfway through our conversation. I tried to stifle my snort, but it escaped.

"Oh hon, this isn't my side of the story. There are court documents that confirm it."

She wanted to see what I had. I sent her a few links to news articles and took photos of the legal documents I had. And then, I realized how shitty I felt. All of the old feelings were coming rushing back—and some I wasn't even aware of. I didn't realize it at that time, but he was manipulative. A bit of a sociopath even. He'd brought out every codependent tendency in my body and, frankly, I wasn't enjoying reliving it.

She had more questions. She wanted to see what else I had. She wanted someone she could commiserate with. And I realized very quickly that someone wasn't me. I mustered every ounce of boundary ability I had at that moment in time, and I voiced my needs.

"I truly do wish you the best. I hope you find peace and a good therapist. This will need to be our last communication. This whole situation is bringing up really bad feelings for me and I don't wish to relive this."

My instinct has always been to protect others, even at the expense of my own well-being. In fact, I've actually put myself out there as a resource for women who have been in a similar situation. But this time I was able to put my own needs first. Can I get a woot woot!?!

I won't call this experience easy, but let's dissect it and discover why it was even "possible:"

- I didn't have a prior relationship with her. She made her own bed (as did I), and now she needed to deal with it.
- It triggered *such* strong emotions. My divorce kicked off a six-month clinical depression. I did not want to go back there. Nay, I *refused* to go back there.
- The more I practice boundary setting, the better I get at it.

In a few moments, you'll have the opportunity to reflect back on some of the times in your life when you've successfully established and upheld a boundary. But first, let's look at how you'll celebrate successes going forward (and some of the positives that might come from it).

I'm a firm believer in celebrating the little wins. Whether it's a happy dance, rewarding yourself with something small, or shouting out "booyah!" and sharing what happened with someone close to you, we need to condition our minds that every boundary set is a victory.

Do you remember the Boundary Hangover chapter and what happened when I stood up for myself with a client? I did a little dance! If I'm being completely honest, I also ran out of my office and into my fiance's. I screamed, "Boundaries Motherclucker!" and then ran back into my office. And no, I didn't say "motherclucker."

Let's look at another example from a few weeks ago. I was at a conference over the summer dedicated to the art and business of professional speaking. I ran into a friend of mine who I've known for years, and she was all excited about a retreat she wanted to put on. She wanted to partner up with my Jiminy Cricket friend and me to put it on.

She was so excited. And as much as I wanted to participate, with every planning call we had, it looked like more and more work was going to fall on my plate. I don't normally shy away from hard work, but with a wedding just a few months away and a book in the works, it probably wasn't the best time for me to take on this responsibility. On top of that, the desired date for the retreat was early January… just a few months away.

With each planning call, I was falling further into a boundary hangover. Until I remembered what my book is about… standing up for yourself, not getting overwhelmed by other people's agendas, and not allowing your time to be hijacked.

I started out small, adding a little devil's advocate to the pot. "I think we need to consider a later date for this event. It's very challenging to get butts in seats, and we want to leave plenty of time to market and get people excited."

My opinion was taken into account, and the date was changed to late spring. But somehow I didn't feel better.

Then, I worked up the nerve to be completely honest. "I hate to be the party pooper here, but I'm taking a course on retreat creation and they recommend against planning it with other speakers. You can bring in another speaker to deliver content, but when you offer too many programs, it does a disservice to the attendees. Honestly, I think you need to make this *your* retreat."

I'm not sure I breathed for a full minute as I waited for her response. I hoped I didn't lose a friend over this, but I had to walk my talk. And then… she surprised the hell out of me.

"Oh, thank you! I've been talking about it with my business coach and she said the same thing. I was just so afraid to upset you ladies after you'd already put time into helping me."

Wait... what? She appreciated me setting a boundary? This was new and exciting. We ended the call, I ran into Tom's office, and let out a "Boundaries, Motherclucker!" (nope, still didn't say "motherclucker"), and then went on with the rest of my day. But wait... there's more.

My Jiminy Cricket friend called me a few hours later. "Thank you so much for saying that. I didn't know how to tell her I don't have time to do this and that I didn't think it was a very good idea."

Well slap my ass and call me Shirley! *Everyone* appreciated my boundary. I slept well that night.

Start out with small boundaries. Politely ask that man on the airplane to move his leg into his leg space and out of yours. Tell the massage therapist that her pressure is too much and you feel like your spleen is about to come shooting out your butt. Practice small and celebrate every victory. The more you do, the better you'll get at it. And the more you point it out to yourself and maybe to a trusted friend, the easier it will become to speak up in the future.

Back To You

1. Now it's time to comb through your history. No doubt there are at least a few times when you've set a boundary. If you can't think of any, check with a boundary buddy. They may recognize them when you don't.

2. Once you've got a handful of boundaries to play with, dissect them. Ask yourself:

   - Why was I comfortable (or at least able to) setting a boundary in this situation and with this person?
   - What was their reaction when I set the boundary?
   - Was there any fallout after the fact?
   - What did I do well?
   - What could I have done better?

3. With all that in mind, it's time to decide how you'll celebrate your victories moving forward. You can choose from the following or make up your own (and probably do these in private so no one thinks you're losing your mind).

   - Yell "Boundaries, Motherclucker!"
   - Make up a saying
   - Fist pump

- High-five the mirror (don't connect—we don't need glass shards everywhere)
- Applaud yourself
- Take a bow
- Sing a few bars of your favorite song (may I recommend "We are the Champions"?)
- Smile and pat yourself on the back
- Phone a friend
- Dance with your dog or cat (while respecting their boundaries)

Chapter 18:

Boundary Backslides

While I'd love to tell you that your unicorn awaits, ready to whisk you off to that magical land with rainbows and healthy boundaries, he's not quite ready to pick you up just yet.

As you travel along this boundary-setting journey, you're going to have some mishaps. I'd imagine that even the most regimented boundary rockstar is going to have the occasional "oops" moment. You will fall. The question is what you'll do to get back up.

There are two aspects to a boundary backslide:

1. Your internal reaction—how you feel about it.
2. Your external reaction—what you do about it.

Let's say, for example, a friend reached out to you to counsel her through (yet another) break up. It's 10 p.m. on a Tuesday. You've got an early client meeting on Wednesday, and you need time in the morning to prepare for it. You know these conversations are never quick, and as much as you want to tell her she'll be fine and you two can unpack this tomorrow afternoon, she just sounds so sad... and she'd be there for you, right? And aren't your friends the most important people in your life? And wouldn't it be selfish of you to leave her high and dry in her time of need?

No, none of those things are true. But it's probably the storm occurring in your head as you bite your lip and settle in for what you know will be two hours of your life that you can never get back.

You spend the next 90-plus minutes reassuring her that there's nothing wrong with her. She just hasn't found the right man yet. He's intimidated by her success. Yada yada yada. And then, you try to go to bed.

"Try" being the key word. You watch the clock, constantly recalculating how much time you'll get to sleep if you go to bed now... now... now.

But you don't get the sleep you need, and you can't believe you did it again. You are supposed to be crushing boundary-setting right now, and this was just a cluster of epic proportions. Maybe you're not cut out for this. Maybe you should accept that your life isn't your own and go back to trying to please everyone. At least that way, you won't be beating yourself up.

Whoa, Nelly! We've all been there (as I shared, I was there last week). The irony is before you knew about boundaries and began your work, you felt resentful and all the other yucky emotions that come from a boundary hangover. But now you feel those AND crappy because you should've known better—you did know better.

It's okay! You had a boundary backslide, and as you work to assert yourself, these are going to happen.

First, stop beating yourself up. Beating yourself up won't help. Shoulda, woulda, coulda… won't help either. The only thing that will? Accepting that you've had a boundary backslide and calling it what it is.

"Oopsie! That was a boundary backslide."

Learning from the Pain

Next, what can you learn from it? Investigate that backslide like a scientist. Ask yourself the following questions:

- With whom did this backslide occur? What is our relationship?
- What (did I feel) was at stake if I upset them?
- What thoughts were running through my head when I agreed to do the thing?

- Were those thoughts true? If not, what was the truth?
- How do I feel in this moment?
- What would have been a more acceptable outcome for me?
- What can I do differently in the future?

There's a movie called *Wanted* with Angelina Jolie. The main character thinks he's suffering from panic attacks but really he's destined to become a highly skilled assassin and his panic attacks are his ability to slow down the world around him. He learns this when he's told to shoot the wings off of flies (poor flies—I know!) and is able to see the individual flaps of their wings.

By investigating a boundary backslide *after the fact,* you are training this muscle so that in the future you can slow time in the moment and make a different choice. No shooting flies required.

Now, let's say that you've agreed to something in the future or more long-term than a two-hour impromptu counseling session. What do you do when you've said yes to something and then realize you've made a horrible mistake?

If you're like me, you HATE going back on your word. If you commit to do something, then come hell or high water you are going to do it. Even if you hate every minute of it. Feel resentful towards the person you supposedly care about. Do a half-assed job because you don't really want to do it. Don't get to do something else that you actually wanted or needed to do to reach your own goals.

Can we cut that shit out now? There's a time and a way to say no when you've already said yes. I have proof... I did it.

Remember earlier when I told you that I agreed to be the president-elect in a professional organization? Well, I'm not the president-elect of that professional organization. After consulting with my therapist, a mentor, Tom, and myself (not in that order), I decided that I'd actually be doing a disservice to myself and to the chapter if I moved forward. Below, I've included the actual email I sent after I made my decision.

> Good Afternoon,
>
> It took a two-hour plane ride with nothing to read for me to truly tap into my heart.
>
> When (President) offered up the possibility of my joining the board and stepping up as President-Elect, I was excited, yet apprehensive. I didn't say yes right away and, instead, took several weeks to process. Wanting to open the door to more speaking opportunities, I

eventually decided that it was a good move for my career.

What I didn't consider was whether it was a good time.

After evaluating everything going on in my life right now (some of it wonderful, some of it very difficult), I've realized that, at this time, I will not be able to serve the chapter the way in which it deserves. I'm grateful I realized this sooner rather than later so someone can step in and provide the leadership the group needs. I would not be bringing my best self to the situation, and you all deserve better.

I am therefore resigning from the board, effective today. I will still be at chapter meetings and am more than happy to assist with setup, being a Buddy, providing PR help, etc. You are all in good hands with (President), and I look forward to serving on the board at some point in the future.

Thank you all for your understanding, your patience, and your service.

A few of the members reached out to check on me and see if they could help in any way. One email stood out in particular (for obvious reasons).

> **Thanks for letting us know now. It's good to have boundaries and even better to articulate them! Thank you and we'll see you on Saturday.**

While I struggled with this decision (and had some FOMO when they announced the new President-Elect), I know I made the best choice. When I think about spending the next two years resenting a role and all of the responsibilities that come along with it, I'm so grateful that I chose this route.

Just because you've agreed to something doesn't mean your decision is set in stone. Now, before you get carried away shirking accepted responsibilities, let's lay some ground rules. In order to change your response, the need to ask yourself the following questions:

- Does the other person have ample time to find a replacement? (Or are you providing an alternative?) If you agreed to drive your friend to the airport at 4 am when Ubers are hard to come by, do not have a change of heart and text her at 3:30 to tell her you just can't help her. That's not fair and will probably result in a missed flight and a lost friendship.

- Do you have a legal responsibility to do what you've agreed to? For example, an attorney can't withdraw from representing a client if it will prejudice the client (make them look bad). Also, you have a legal responsibility if you signed a contract and the other party is relying on you to get something done within a specific amount of time.

If you have reviewed the above conditions and feel that changing your answer is indeed the right move for everyone involved, it's time to communicate that. Here are a few tips for softening the blow.

- State your new answer clearly and assertively. The worst thing you can do now is make people guess as to what's happening. Here's an example of how to word your refusal: "When I agreed to help you with X, I believed that I would be able to handle the extra responsibilities. After looking at my schedule/workload/etc., I've determined that I have overextended myself." Depending on the relationship, you may want to provide a reason. However, it's not a requirement.
- It's not you, it's me. Take a queue from the world's most famous breakup line. Let them know that you would not be able to handle the responsibilities properly and would be doing a disservice to them if you continued

on. Heading back to our earlier example of the 10 p.m. call for help, you are not a therapist (unless you are). Either way, you are not your friend's therapist, and while you can be there to lend an ear, you cannot provide an actual counseling session. It would be irresponsible and inappropriate. Communicating this might look like, "While I want to support you through difficult times, I am not qualified to provide the therapy you are looking for."

- Create an alternative. If you truly want to be of assistance in this situation, tap into your Improv skills and utilize the "Yes, And" process here. Perhaps you need to propose a new timeline. "I can still help you, however, I need to finish planning my husband's surprise party first." Or maybe you can handle *a piece* of a project rather than the whole thing. "I'd still be happy to drive you to the airport; however, I've already got plans when you fly back into town and need you to find someone else to pick you up." Or maybe, you can suggest someone else who can do the thing instead of you. For example, mid-pandemic I was introduced to someone looking for blog content. He was a Personal Protective Equipment (PPE) Broker (yep, that's a thing). Apparently, royalty in the Middle East was buying up gloves, masks, and other personal protective equipment and then using brokers to sell them (at a higher price) to hospitals and other medical facilities. My first reaction was, "It's not exactly my passion, but it could be a good-paying project," and I offered to get him a quote for weekly blogs. The moment I got off the call, my reaction shifted to, "How can that guy sleep at night!? And how will I sleep at night if I work for this man?" I called a friend who runs a larger content-creation company with writers in every industry, checked to see if she could handle it, and within five minutes, I was back on the phone with him. "I appreciate the opportunity, however, it's not what I specialize in. I've already spoken with another content writer and she can help you." I thought it was best to leave out the part about my skin crawling and not wanting to shit all over my moral compass.

- Apologize. The last thing you want to do is damage a relationship with someone you care about, which means an, "I'm sorry for letting you down" may be in order. Mind you, saying no to the creepy PPE Broker does not warrant an apology. However, for those relationships you'd like to maintain, consider apologizing and expressing your gratitude for their understanding.
- Leave the door open (but only if you want to). In some cases, what they asked of you was not the problem, but rather *when*. In that situation, you can let them know that

you appreciate them thinking of you and, while you can't help this time, you'd appreciate it if they'd keep you in mind in the future. If you expect your load to lighten during a specific time frame, you can tell them to check back in six months or whatever works with your schedule.

- Do better next time. Head up to that "Learning from the Pain" exercise and realize that even though you've had a boundary backslide, the best thing you can do moving forward is learn from it so it doesn't happen again.

If you haven't picked up on the theme of this chapter yet, it's that Boundary Backslides will happen. You will say yes when you really want to say no. Thankfully, you can learn from the situation, and depending on the specifics, you can even change your yes to a no. In most cases, relationships will not be destroyed. But don't worry if they are, we're going to talk about that in the next chapter.

Interview with Jamie Lee – Animal Reiki Practitioner and Owner of Animal-Bonds

Where do you think your boundaries originated?

Well, definitely not in childhood. My father had a personality disorder/mental illness and lacked empathy. He could be emotionally cold and controlling, and I constantly lived in fear of upsetting him. I learned to become invisible—figured I couldn't get in trouble if I blended in. As so many children of alcoholics do, I married an alcoholic/drug addict. I was a partier too, but I was ready to clean up my life. He wasn't. He was distant and self-destructive.

I spent months curled up and crying every night and eventually began to hope that he just wouldn't come home. We'd had a lot of fun together in the past, which made leaving him even harder. I think that's why it can be so hard to set boundaries with people. We remember the good times, and then when we leave, we only remember the bad. But there is a balance.

During that time, I sought help in ALANON and had an amazing sponsor who really worked the program. It was like therapy with homework. I learned how to stand up for myself. That's when I realized I am responsible for my own happiness—no one else is.

I'd love to say that all of a sudden I had perfect boundaries, but that's not how it works. Baby steps. And usually, it's two steps forward and one step back. I did a lot of different therapies, took a grief recovery class, and then I discovered reiki. It was the first step on my spiritual path. It's so important that you have some sort of spiritual practice, whether it's organized religion, meditation, or even just a daily gratitude practice. This is when you learn to truly respect yourself and others. When someone invades your boundaries, you can lovingly say no.

This came in handy when I worked for the county. There was a culture of working overtime. Employees would get up at 2 a.m., work a full day's shift and then stay on to work overtime at night. It wasn't written anywhere, but there was constant pressure to do more. When you didn't, you were labeled as a slacker or lazy. Well, there was "mandatory overtime" on New Year's Eve. I heard through the grapevine that since I never worked overtime, I was being targeted for this shift. I did my research and looked into what would happen if I refused. It turned out the punishment for not working overtime... was that you couldn't work overtime. I laughed and thought, "I can handle that."

Are there any beliefs you had to bust through to get where you are now?

I was born in 1959, a time when women rarely worked outside of the home. We were taught from an early age that we had to take care of everyone. It was our responsibility. Get married. Have kids. Run the home. Thankfully, I had a great role model. My mom worked as a nurse and assured me that I could do that, but only if I wanted to. It was good to hear, but it didn't drown out the expectations society put on me. The world told me how I was supposed to behave.

How do you weigh "opportunities" when they're presented?

Knowing who you are and what matters to you is essential. Whenever I'm asked to do something, I never answer right away. Instead, I step away, take the time to quiet my mind, sit in stillness, and meditate.

I ask myself, "Is this in alignment with who I am?"

Then, I have to be realistic with my time. I used to live with every moment accounted for. I can't do that anymore. I need downtime. If I don't have time to recharge, I'm not my creative best.

I could let the fear of missing out get in the way, but if I go somewhere or do something I don't really want to do, I'm just going to be resentful. And that's not fun for anyone.

What do women need to know as they begin their boundary journey?

Live a life that's in alignment with who you are. Don't try to be who the world tells you to be.

Back to You

1. Think of a boundary backslide you've had recently. Apply the "Learning from your Pain" process.
2. Are there any areas in your life where you've had a boundary backslide, but still have the opportunity to make it right? If so, make a decision and then communicate that decision to the other party.

Chapter 19:

Saying Goodbye to Boundary Busters

It took a while after my divorce and my move to Vegas to be ready for a full-time job. It was around 2009, and I was coming out of the depression and beginning to pull my life back together. I was doing better, but a 9-5 wasn't the least bit appealing or necessary during my healing journey.

When a new friend told me about a company that provided nannies to families staying in the hotels, I figured it might be the perfect opportunity to make a little money while avoiding long-term responsibility and full-time stress. I could hang out with kids for a few hours a day and pay the few bills I had at the moment.

Older kids, that is. Sure, I did the babysitting thing when I was a teenager but, being an only child I was never surrounded by babies. Truth be told, I don't have the slightest idea how to care for a baby. I don't know how to feed them, change a diaper, or get them to stop crying. Not. My. Wheelhouse. If they couldn't wipe their own butt, I was out.

Thankfully, the company was very clear that they respected boundaries. If you wanted to work with a specific age group that was great. They would make it happen. If you could only work certain hours or days that was perfect. Speak up about your wants and your needs, and they would be upheld.

Until they needed something.

I remember the night clearly. I was all settled in for the evening. Jammies on, contacts out, when I got the phone call.

"We need you to do a last-minute job."

I looked down at my PJs. I was so comfy. But I didn't want to disappoint them. If I said no would they think of me for the next available job or would my name disappear from the roster?

"Ummm... I guess I could do it," I said sheepishly.

"Great! It's a six-year-old and a two-year-old at Planet Hollywood. You'll need to be there at 8 pm."

My heart dropped into my stomach. There was no chance a two-year-old was taking care of their own potty situation. "I can't watch a two-year-old. I don't know how to take care of them."

"You'll be fine. She's going to be sleeping. We need you."

Three hours later, I found myself sitting on the floor of a hotel room, with a crying two-year-old wrapped around me. She had woken up in the middle of the night and had a meltdown (understandably) because her parents were nowhere to be seen. Oh, and did I mention she had Autism?

Thankfully, we both survived the night. I worked for the company for another three months until I received a similar call. I was grateful that nothing worse had happened that first night, and frankly, I wasn't willing to tempt fate. As it became obvious that they only respected boundaries when it suited them, I decided the job was no longer a good fit for me.

As comfortable and proficient as we become at setting boundaries, there will always be those who:

- Don't like our new assertiveness.
- Refuse to respect our boundaries.

Because of this, there will come a time when we must make a choice: are we willing to go back to our old way of people-pleasing, martyrdom, and being unwilling to stand up for ourselves and our needs or will we need to say goodbye to some of our relationships?

Hopefully, you read that last paragraph and said, "What the duck? That first option is never gonna happen! I'm a boundary rockstar now and I'm never going back!"

All that being said, let's take a look at what you can expect (and accept) along this journey, and what should have you saying, "No Mas!" to the boundary busters in your life.

What to Expect When You're Boundary Setting

You, my friend, are about to upset the apple cart. Your friends, family, coworkers, boss, and clients—they're all nice and comfortable. They know that when they ask you to do something or go somewhere, no matter how much it inconveniences you, you're going to say yes. They know they can count on you for the late-night bitchfests, the rooster's-buttcrack-of-dawn rides to the airport, the last-minute project that *just has to get done this weekend*, and any other "favor" they can think of.

And you've just said no.

Some of the people in your life will get a little smirk on their face, understanding what's just happened. They've been waiting years for you to establish boundaries and they couldn't be prouder.

Some… but not most.

Most will do a double take. Maybe they didn't even register what you said and just kept going. Maybe they laughed, thinking you were just kidding. Maybe they even touched the spot where your face meets your neck and tried to pull, thinking it's someone else wearing a mask of your face or you've just been body snatched.

Either way, you just threw them for a huge fricking loop. You've turned their happy little world upside down by standing up for yourself, and frankly, they don't know what to do with themselves.

Truthfully, you can't expect people not to have any issues whatsoever with your newfound strength. You've spent the last how-many years training them on how to treat you, and you've done a standup job. Now, you'll need to retrain them. It's doable, but it's going to take some patience.

According to *Set Boundaries, Find Peace*, you're likely to encounter a number of different behaviors when you first begin setting boundaries:

- Pushback. They'll ignore your boundary and keep on keeping on.
- Testing Limits. They'll get sneaky, trying to get one past you. This is like pushback but on the sly.

- Rationalizing and Questioning. They want to know why you've got this boundary and is it truly valid.
- Defensiveness. They'll turn the tables, making excuses about how the issue is actually yours and not their behavior.
- Silent Treatment. In the hopes that you'll fold and give up your boundary, they'll stop talking to you.

Stay strong. Realize that these tactics are their ego's way of attempting to return to the status quo. Change is scary and they're going to do everything they can to go back to their nice comfy existence—you know, the one where you do their shit before your own.

As you restate your boundary, continue to uphold it, and let their comments roll off your back (as I mentioned in *Surviving to Thriving*, sometimes you have to be a duck); they're going to accept the new normal.

Or they won't.

There will be people in your life who refuse to accept version You 2.0. They will continue to push. They will make you feel like the worst human in the world. And, if you're lucky, they'll do the work for you and drop out of your life.

I never finished the story about my existential crisis last winter. My body and my soul forced me to set boundaries. Without them, I wouldn't have survived another six months. I couldn't/wouldn't continue the schedule I was keeping, the availability I promised, the insufficient income I was making. I set a boundary. And I got laid off. Maybe the universe knew that I wasn't prepared to uphold those boundaries. Maybe my boss even knew it. Either way, the job "dropped out of my life."

Most of the time, you're going to have to pull that trigger yourself. When it becomes evident that certain people in your life are not willing or capable of respecting your boundaries, it's time to say goodbye.

My friend Allison (name has been changed) was seeing a guy for almost a year. She was unsure of the relationship for a while, but when they went away for a week-long vacation, her mind was made up. He was not the man for her.

As many of us do (soooo guilty over here), she agreed to be friends with him after the fact. To her, friends meant a few quick texts during the week and maybe grabbing lunch once a month or so. To him, friends meant they'd talk daily, see each other multiple times per week, and she'd be his primary (okay, only) source of support as his mother was fighting brain cancer.

It was too much for Allison. With a full-time job, full-time school, and applying to graduate school, she didn't have the emotional bandwidth or the time that he was looking for. She'd explained it (in very plain English), but he always wanted more. This went on for almost two years. When she'd take a step back, he'd berate her, saying she was selfish and a horrible friend. When she'd loosen up on her boundaries and try to make him happy, he behaved… until the next time she couldn't meet his demand.

When she finally put her foot down and said they could no longer be in each other's lives, he ghosted her for two weeks and then reappeared with, "Can we talk? I have a few things I need to say before we're out of each other's lives for good."

If you're sitting there screaming at the book like watching the co-ed go into the dark basement in a horror movie, you're not alone. Myself and another friend were watching this in real-time and could clearly see the killer hiding in the shadows. But that's how it is when you're on the outside looking in. With no emotional attachment, no fear of being ostracized from the tribe and eaten, and no need to "be nice," it's really easy to point out what needs to happen.

So we just tried to be supportive. She talked to her therapist, and thank goodness, they worked through it: the ex is emotionally manipulative and

Allison owes him nothing. She's letting him know that they are done communicating. Then, she'll block all contact.

How to Say Goodbye

Before we dive into this I want to reiterate I am not a therapist. This book is not an alternative to professional help, and if you are in physical danger, you need to find a professional who can help you create an exit strategy. If you have a dangerous individual in your life and you do fear for your safety, there's no amount of boundary setting that's going to make it okay. Once you're in a safe place and getting professional guidance, you can finish reading this.

And, we're back!

You have the right to exorcize anyone from your life. Whether you've gotten into a toxic romantic relationship, had a friendship "forever," worked with a boss who refuses to respect your time off, or have a parent who constantly puts you down and abuses their power. Yes, you can even remove a parent from your life. I know they gave you life. They raised you. You can't possibly turn your back.

Yeah. You can. I'm not saying you should disavow all knowledge because your loving mother refused to adhere to your "fewer presents for Christmas" rule with your kids. I'm saying that when your parents are abusive, toxic, and add nothing but pain and suffering to your life, you need to step out of the tormented child role and make a change to protect yourself.

Not ready to put a permanent end to your relationship? Hit pause. Take a step back physically and emotionally. Put some distance between yourself and those toxic people while you do your inner work. When you are stronger and more prepared to handle their dysfunction, consider adding them back in on a limited and temporary basis.

You can handle this goodbye in one of two ways.

1. Let the other person know why (repeated boundary violations) you can no longer have them in your life.
2. Ghost them. You leave the relationship and cut off all contact without letting them know.

While number one may seem more difficult in the short term (no one likes to have these conversations), it's like ripping a bandaid off quickly. Option number two may seem easier since you don't actually have to confront them, but it could drag the situation out as they search for closure through any means necessary (i.e., harassing every friend and family member of yours, showing up at your job, blowing up your social media, etc.).

As I've built my writing business, I've encountered some boundary busters. While I didn't know how to communicate boundaries to (or have any with) my clients in the beginning, I've learned the hard way. And let me tell you, you haven't lived until you've fired a client.

A good client of mine referred a ghostwriting prospect to me a few years ago. Our initial call went well and I agreed to work with him. It went downhill from there. He didn't pay on time. He called and texted me (I only have a personal phone) on weekends, and since he was in a different time zone, he saw nothing wrong with shooting off a text at 6 am my time on a Sunday. This was before I knew about the power of Do Not Disturb so he woke me up every Sunday for about two months.

I began to establish some boundaries:

- No texts on weekends or before 9 am or after 5 pm any day.
- Invoices must be paid before work begins for the month.

I had established boundaries. But, it turned out that I didn't know how to uphold them yet. When I was three weeks into the current month and still hadn't been paid, I wrote him a long email making my case. I was trying to work with him but it was disrespectful that he wasn't paying me on time… yada, yada, yada.

I read it to Jen, my attorney friend, before hitting Send.

"That's really well written, Sheryl. Nice job."

I beamed with pride.

"Now delete the whole thing."

Wait. What?

"Type the following sentence: 'No more work will be done until past invoices are paid in full.' Now hit Send."

My entire being was cringing but I did it. I received an email back almost immediately. "I'll pay the invoice on Monday."

Phew! I wiped the imaginary sweat from my brow. It was Friday. I'd have my money by Monday. I was sitting on my couch the next day enjoying some quality Netflix and cuddle time with my puppy. My phone buzzed. It was him. And it was a LOOOOONG text about all the things we should add to the next chapter.

I called my attorney friend for some external courage, but I knew what I had to do. I marched up to my office, attached the work-in-progress to an email and added a note. "After repeated requests that you respect my boundaries, I've determined that we are not a good fit for one another. I will not continue to ghostwrite your book. I've attached what I've written so far and I wish you luck in finding a good fit."

Hasta la vista, baby.

Sometimes relationships just aren't a good fit, and it's time to end them.

To be clear, releasing someone from your life doesn't mean you don't care about them. What it does mean is that you care about you. You are (for the first time ever) putting your needs first and that is admirable. You can release them with love and grieve for the loss while knowing you've done the right thing.

Yes, setting boundaries can be challenging. It can be confusing to the people in your life who are used to you doing whatever they ask. However, if you have a healthy relationship with a healthy individual, setting boundaries will only strengthen your relationship. It will never destroy it.

Back to You

1. As you begin to set boundaries, what reactions have you seen from the people in your life?
2. How have you handled these reactions?
3. Are there any people who have outright refused to respect your newfound strength?
4. Consider how you may remove them from your life.

Conclusion

There she is my boundary-building friend. Your very own unicorn to whisk you off to the land of healthy boundaries. She's small, but she'll get the job done.

First, let me say congratulations. This journey is rough and it can truly suck at times. My friend likened it to a detox—it's "an awful feeling process that you've gotta go through to get to the good feelings on the other side."

I'd love to tell you that with the arrival of your unicorn, those icky feelings will never again surface. But, I'd be lying. As you read in the interviews with Boundary Rock Stars, you are going to have backslides. You will accept "opportunities" that turn out to be nothing but time sucks. You will take two steps forward and one step back. You will lose some of the people in your life. That's probably the hardest part about all of this—but it's also the most valuable.

In feng shui, it's believed that when you get rid of the old, stale shit that's taking up physical space and energetic space in your life, you make room for the good stuff. Yeah, I don't think a wise, old Asian person ever put it quite like that, but you get my drift. There are people in your life who don't deserve to be there. They don't treat you nicely. They don't respect you. And frankly, they are just taking up space. Set your boundaries. Uphold your boundaries. Those people will show themselves the door... and they'll open up space for new, amazing people to come in.

Finally, you are not a victim. People have not taken advantage of your boundaries. You have *allowed* your boundaries to be taken advantage of. What's the distinction? Well in the former, if it happened once, it can happen again. After all, you don't have control over your reality. In the latter, you have all the control. If you have previously allowed people to poop all over your wants/needs/expectations, then you can make the decision not to anymore. Declare your life a no-poop zone (except for that unicorn... nature and all) and start demanding better.

You are worth it.

If you'd like some help along your boundary journey, make sure you sign up for my newsletter at www.YouHadMeAtNo.com to be notified of upcoming events and programs.

Meet the Author

Yes. Of course. I'd be happy to. It's no problem at all.

Sheryl Green has taken "people-pleasing" to Olympic levels. For decades, she put everyone else's needs above her own... until she hit a metaphorical brick wall.

After committing to one-too-many responsibilities, Sheryl discovered the importance of boundaries.... Okay, she actually discovered that boundaries were even "a thing." Now she works with individuals and organizations to establish healthy boundaries to improve relationships, communication, and well-being.

"Goth" as a teenager, Sheryl dreamed of being an FBI Profiler and hunting down serial killers. She earned a Master's Degree in Forensic Psychology, but decided against spending her days in the minds of serial killers and instead has worked in Mental Health, Customer Service, Public Relations, Education, and the Nonprofit world, bringing a unique blend of experience and insight to her audiences.

Sheryl is the author of six books (of her own), including *Surviving to Thriving: How to Overcome Setbacks and Rock Your Life; Once Upon a Bottom Line: Harnessing the Power of Storytelling in Sales*;

Book Writing For Busy People; *Do Good to Do Better: The Small Business Guide to Growing Your Business by Helping Nonprofits*; *A Pet Parent's Guide to First Aid and Prevention*; and her latest, *You Had Me at No: How Setting Healthy Boundaries Banishes Burnout, Repairs Relationships, and Saves Your Sanity*.

She is also an avid animal advocate, dedicating her life to providing a voice for those who cannot speak. She previously served as the Director of Communications and Cuddling for a local animal rescue and continues to donate her time, talent, and money to animal welfare organizations.

When she's not working, she's spending time with her husband and their two fur babies, doing yoga, and tending to a small jungle's worth of houseplants.

To hire Sheryl or learn more about her programs and books, visit www.sherylgreenspeaks.com.

Philanthropy

Throughout this book, you've learned about some of the ways animals have impacted my life. The one common thread? With every single life I saved, they saved me right back.

Animals can't speak for themselves, which is why I've dedicated my platform to being their voice. 5% of every sale from my books and my speaking engagements goes to local animal rescues. Some of these include:

Vegas Pet Rescue Project is a 501(c)3 organization working to positively impact the Las Vegas homeless, abused, and abandoned pets that overwhelm our shelter system by giving them a new lease on LIFE. In addition, they help finance spay and neuter programs to help low-income families be responsible pet owners and to decrease the overpopulation issues we face in Vegas. Learn more at Vegaspetrescueproject.org.

Vegas Cat Rescue is a 501(c)3 organization that is working to reduce the ever-growing feral and stray cat population (200,000+). Their program provides medical attention (including spay and neuter), food, and whenever possible, a forever home for these cats and kittens. Their long-term goal is to create a sanctuary so the rescued cats can live their lives in a safe environment. Learn more at vegascatrescue.org.

Acknowledgments

I couldn't have written this book without all of the wonderful people (and animals) in my life.

Thank you to my beta readers for digging through a very messy first draft: Alex Bratty, Misty Weltzien, Jen Braster, Jen Espinosa, Julie Smith, Candace Medina, Kathy Kulesza, Mark Levy, and Emily Lewis. And to my interview subjects, Chris Williams, Michelle Miller, Alex Bratty, Jen Braster, Jamie Lee, Katie Perry, and Jennifer Scher for sharing their insights and their stories.

Taryn Wittenwiler, thank you for editing my work. I still think you should charge by the comma.

Stephanie Feger, thank you for your marketing guidance.

Thank you to my parents for their love and support and for punishing me in the fourth grade by taking TV away and making me read. I wouldn't be the writer I am today without you.

Earl Bell, thank you for giving me permission to do what's right.

Bodhi and Buddy, thank you for serving as Quality Control and snoozing soundly while I wrote. I aspire to reach your level of peace and contentment.

Last (but certainly not least), thank you to Tom Freeman, my husband, my rock, my sounding board, and my favorite weirdo. This book wouldn't have happened without your encouragement, support, and eye-opening conversations. I love you and I look forward to helping you retire.

Resources

Aron, Elaine. *The Highly Sensitive Person: How to Thrive When the World Overwhelms You*. New York, Thorsons, 1997.

De Becker, Gavin. *The Gift of Fear: And Other Survival Signals That Protect Us from Violence*. New York, Dell, 1997. Reprint, Toronto: Little Brown and Company, 1998.

Burkeman, Oliver. *Four Thousand Weeks: Time Management for Mortals*. New York, Farrar, Straus and Giroux, 2021.

Cole, Terri. *Boundary Boss: The Essential Guide to Talk True, Be Seen, and (Finally) Live Free*. 1st ed. Colorado, Sounds True, 2021.
"Boundary Boss" © 2021 Terri Cole quoted with permission from the publisher, Sounds True Inc.

Huffington, Arianna. *Thrive: The Third Metric to Redefining Success and Creating a Life of Well-Being, Wisdom, and Wonder*. New York, Harmony, 2014.

Kilgariff, Karen, and Georgia Hardstark. *Stay*

Sexy & Don't Get Murdered: The Definitive How-To Guide. New York, Tom Doherty Associates, 2019.

De Azevedo Hanks, Julie. *The Assertiveness Guide for Women: How to Communicate Your Needs, Set Healthy Boundaries, and Transform Your Relationships.* Oakland, New Harbinger Publications, 2016.

Mellody, Pia. *Facing Codependence: What It Is, Where It Comes from, How It Sabotages Our Lives.* 1st ed. New York, Harper & Row, 2003.

Pacheco, Rebecca, "Learning to Hear the Voice of Self-Care." *Yoga Journal*, Issue Number 327, Summer 2022

Sincero, Jen. *Badass Habits: Cultivate the Awareness, Boundaries, and Daily Upgrades You Need to Make Them Stick.* London: Penguin Life, 2020.

Tawwab, Nedra Glover. *Set Boundaries, Find Peace: A Guide to Reclaiming Yourself.* New York, TarcherPerigee, 2021.

Aron, Elaine. "The Highly Sensitive Person Quiz" 2023. https://hsperson.com/test/highly-sensitive-test/

Klein, Joey. "Inner Matrix Systems." 2023.
https://innermatrixsystems.com/ *For a
discount on your first class, call the
office at (720) 446-5533 and mention my
name.

Brophy, Topher. "The Tree Who Set Healthy
Boundaries." 2022.
https://www.topherpayne.com/giving-tre
e

Mark, Gloria. The Cost of Interrupted Work: More
Speed and Stress
https://www.ics.uci.edu/~gmark/chi08-mark.
pdf

Martin, Dr. Sharon. "13 Signs You Grew up in

an Enmeshed Family." Live Well with

Sharon Martin, 9 Oct. 2021,
www.livewellwithsharonmartin.com/enm
eshment/

Made in the USA
Middletown, DE
28 May 2024

54817212R00157